D0726113

THE KOREAN-AMERICAN DREAM

THE KOREAN-AMERICAN DREAM

Portraits of a Successful Immigrant Community

JAMES FLANIGAN

UNIVERSITY OF NEVADA PRESS *Reno & Las Vegas*

University of Nevada Press | Reno, Nevada 89557 USA
www.unpress.nevada.edu
Copyright © 2018 by University of Nevada Press
All rights reserved
Cover photographs © iStock / voyata
Cover design by Martyn Schmoll

LIBRARY OF CONGRESS CATALOGING-IN-PUBLICATION DATA
Names: Flanigan, James, 1936– author.
Title: The Korean-American dream : portraits of a successful immigrant community/
    James Flanigan.
Description: First edition. | Reno, Nevada : University of Nevada Press, [2018] |
    Includes bibliographical references and index. |
Identifiers: LCCN 2018013987 (print) | LCCN 2018017090 (e-book) |
    ISBN 978-1-943859-85-6 (pbk. : alk. paper) | ISBN 978-1-943859-86-3 (e-book)
Subjects: LCSH: Korean Americans—California—Los Angeles. | Korean Americans—
    Social conditions. | Korean Americans—Economic conditions. | Koreans—United
    States—Emigration and immigration. | Koreans—United States—History.
Classification: LCC E184.K6 (e-book) | LCC E184.K6 F55 2018 (print) |
    DDC 979.4/94004957—dc23
LC record available at https://lccn.loc.gov/2018013987

The paper used in this book meets the requirements of American National
Standard for Information Sciences—Permanence of Paper for Printed Library
Materials, ANSI/NISO Z39.48-1992 (R2002).

FIRST PRINTING

Manufactured in the United States of America

To Patricia and Anne (R.I.P.) and our families.

Contents

Preface

Yang Ho Cho said the Wilshire Grand Tower is an "icon of the Korean community for Los Angeles." Cho is chairman of Korean Air and its parent company Hanjin Shipping, which have built a major presence in L.A. over forty-five years. Cho himself, son of the founder of Hanjin, came here in 1974 when he was twenty-five to lead Korean Air's operations. At his direction the companies have invested more than $1 billion to build the new landmark Wilshire Grand Hotel and office building—tallest in the West—in downtown Los Angeles.

But this book and Cho's emotive words on "Korean Community" are about more than business. They are about the society and culture, the struggles and contributions, of Korean immigrants and their families over the last century, people who have made Los Angeles the largest Korean city outside of Seoul and who have contributed significantly to New York and northern New Jersey, Chicago, Atlanta, Houston, and other cities across the country. This book tells of their Korean culture and history and, as important, how they renew us by adapting to our American culture of "E Pluribus Unum," one from many, a new, diverse concept of a nation.

I have come to know Korean Americans in many corners of the United States and the world over four decades of reporting and writing about them as businesspeople and teachers, soldiers and doctors, individuals and families. Some in this book have appeared in others; many more I have met and interviewed in four years of research for this book. Even before that, I recall being fascinated in 1980 to learn that South Korea produced more computer chips than the entire Soviet Union. Also I met Korean construction workers in 1975 in newly oil-rich Saudi Arabia, when they came on contract to build Riyadh from an oasis into a city. With customary energy, Korean workers were doing calisthenics at dawn before starting on their desert project.

But final impetus to produce this book occurred in 2014 when Chairman Cho said the landmark he was authorizing would stand as an icon of the Korean Community for Los Angeles. Cho said he wanted the tower to serve as a symbol for community members and their children to take pride in their success as immigrants. He spoke of immigrants "who came here and started businesses and learned trades."[1] He called Los Angeles a "microcosm of the United States—a land built of immigrants who want to do one thing: improve their lives."[2] I shook his hand that evening and said I would write a book about that community.

And so this book came together as fates have brought South and North Korea to the brink of war—or peace—and brought all Americans to a time of critical difference and debates about immigration, citizenship, and involvement in the global community. To all those questions, Koreans demonstrate the promise of the American mosaic. That's why I call them a beacon for the future.

Big thoughts! Bold statements, dear readers. But I hear you ask, why Koreans? Are they different from other immigrants? No, not really, though as a relatively small group compared to communities from China, the Philippines, and India, they have shown uncommon eagerness to secure what they call a "seat at the table" in the American community.

Of course, Koreans and Americans do share a history of a modern state founded by the U.S. military in 1945 at the close of World War II and sealed in blood of the Korean War, 1950–53. Koreans are a reminder of the struggles of immigrants who built America over some 250 years. Those who have come before were mostly from Europe and of course from Africa, under different circumstances. Thus the Korean community adds to the variety of people and talent in L.A. and nationwide. And it is always people and talent that make great institutions, whether company or club, university or agency—or indeed build a city, a state, a nation.

This book will tell all that in stories of people. The woman who as a young girl walked with her mother down through battlefields from North to South Korea during the Korean War and came ultimately to Chicago and then Southern California, where she and her husband built a fine business.

It will tell of the pioneer who defined the original vision of Korean American and whose daughter became the first Asian American officer in the U.S. military and later a leader of the California community, living to a hundred years. And it will tell of the hero who fought in

World War II and the Korean War and then started organizations to help youth and families in the Korean community.

Immigrants to America have always formed clubs to sing sentimental songs of the old country, to play cards and form community, but Koreans from early on formed organizations to lobby for political causes and resolutions—notably the Network of Korean American Leaders in 2006 at the University of Southern California and the Council of Korean Americans in 2011, which now holds annual summits in Washington, DC.

But this is not a book about a "model minority," an offensive term to all minorities because it makes race the essential point, encourages stereotypes, and overlooks individual achievement. I see Korean Americans as a community of immigrants, their offspring and descendants with the same anxieties and troubles that other groups have endured.

Jihee Huh, a prominent Korean American, defines her people: "We are a very eclectic people with many talents but most importantly focus on education and hard work as our collective mantra." Her reference to education reflects the history of a class system in Korea that denied education to all but the aristocracy or Yangban class. Since Korea survived Japanese colonization and became a newly independent country at the end of World War II, its people have become fierce about education. We'll read of Jihee Huh in two chapters of this seven-chapter book, as we'll read of many other Korean leaders, thinkers, innovators, and organizers.

In chapter 2, I'll explain the Immigration and Nationality Act of 1965 that brought so many Koreans and other Asian people here, launching the new Pacific Age of America.

Immigration is an important theme in this book. It is not a mere sentiment nor even a political argument, but hard reality. Immigrants are needed because some 73 percent of U.S. industries report labor shortages and 55 percent call labor shortages a major problem.[3]

And it is a Korean problem because an estimated 10,000 Korean immigrants are DACA, or deferred action for childhood arrivals. "Immigration is a family affair in the Korean community," says Sam Yoon, executive director of the Council of Korean Americans (CKA). The council is working to gain legislation that will protect DACA youths so they may earn Green Cards, for continued access to the country, and ultimately U.S. citizenship.

Immigration is always about the future of America. My own mother and father immigrated from Ireland decades ago with only six or seven years of education and worked hard loading trucks in warehouses and in domestic service. But their son received a good education and access to work and better living, as children of immigrants have always done. The difference is independence. In old countries, Korean and otherwise, culture and tradition rule. You are who generations of forebears say you are. But in America, you are on your own; you can think anew and act anew. That can be unsettling but also invigorating. "Immigrants are 100 times more likely to start a business," says John Suh, chief executive of LegalZoom, Inc., a son of immigrants from Korea in a company founded by a Korean immigrant.

Another theme is the American West in a new Pacific Age. That is not some misty travel idea but historic reality, with 60 percent of the world's population living in Asia—37 percent of the world in China and India together. Los Angeles is not the "West Coast," as it is always called, but the Eastern Shore of a vast Pacific World, which sends visitors and goods, people and new ideas through the seaports and airports of California.

This book talks of challenge: The L.A. Riots of 1992 that resulted in several deaths, 2,300 Korean stores being burned out, and a profound indifference to the Korean community's plight by police and public officials. And Response: A great burst of organizing and reaching out among the Koreans in L.A. and across the United States that helped bring the community to where it is today. We'll read of the lawyer who gathered eighty Korean American lawyers on the night of the riots to help store owners understand the language of contracts, leases, and laws to help them.

Today there is a feeling among many L.A. folks that Koreans came here with money, and that is why they own businesses and have real estate and so forth. But no, they came relatively penniless but with a system of pooling resources—pooling the money in *kehs*—to start ventures, many of which failed, leaving the family not only broke but obligated to pay the other keh members back. We'll read in chapter 3 of entrepreneurs in the fashion industry who lost fortunes in the early 1990s and of the son who helped his parents pay their pooled investors back and then founded his own apparel firm that has become a noted fashion brand.

We'll also read of a Korean immigrant, a medical doctor, who organized investment in the post–Cold War recession to buy office buildings in Los Angeles, and of his daughter and son, who now are converting office properties to residential.

And we'll read of a young immigrant couple who opened a store in L.A., called Fashion 21, selling apparel to teens and young women in 1984. Three decades later Forever 21 is the largest worldwide purveyor of fashion to young women, and its owner says reverently "all of this was started by a simple immigrant with a dream."[4] Indeed, with new companies starting up to design and sell their fashions online, Los Angeles County, with more than 100,000 employees, ranks first in the United States in apparel and related industries.

Korean entrepreneurs also have joined the American tradition of giving back, to universities and hospitals and churches and social causes. And that has had an effect. So, to answer the readers' question:

Why Koreans? Because universities across America now have departments of Korean Studies, from Harvard, Yale, Columbia, and Penn in the East, to the Universities of Michigan, Chicago, Indiana, and Ohio State in the Midwest, to Stanford, UC Berkeley, UC Riverside, UC Irvine, UCLA, USC, and many more. One reason is that the government of South Korea, with its economy rising in 1991, formed the Korea Foundation to promote the study of Korean culture.

Why Koreans? Because K-Pop music enthralls the young, and Korean dramas even more significantly rank high in television markets in Indonesia, Vietnam, China, Japan, Iran, and Africa, from Ghana and Nigeria in the west to Kenya, Tanzania and Zimbabwe in the east. Now Korean entertainment, based in L.A., hopes to make great strides in the big U.S. market. We'll look at that in chapter 7 of the book.

Why Koreans? Because the 1,500 Korean churches in greater Los Angeles—4,500 nationwide—are a social and political powerhouse. Denominations are largely Presbyterian, Methodist, and Baptist. The Catholic Church also produces many priests from Korea and the Korean American community. Hyepin Im, president of Faith and Community Empowerment (formerly named Korean Churches for Community Development), talks of "leveraging the power base of the churches through the Pan Asian Faith community to lobby for education and help for people to obtain housing, community centers, family services."[5]

To get a sense of why the Korean community has so warmly made Los Angeles its home, referring to L.A. as an "eastern district of Seoul" and "Capital of the Pacific Rim," listen to a sophisticated woman who immigrated from Korea when she was seventeen. Sabrina Kay founded California Design College in 1991 to train young people for the apparel trade. She sold that school for considerable money, earned several more academic degrees, and now owns Fremont University, which trains people for work in law offices or health and fitness centers and other aspects of business and design. Her contrast to society in her homeland is instructive.

"I think my second career is to give opportunity back to America which gave opportunity to me," she declares. And then she turns up the volume. "There is no country like America that gives opportunity to almost anybody without social connections or ranking systems," she declares. "You don't have to be born into an upper class to succeed. This country gives opportunity to everybody and anybody. There is no country like this!"[6]

Finally, as Korean Americans have achieved success in their new country, they are acting for the old country as immigrants from Europe have always done, and immigrants from Asia do now in Vietnam and China as well as Korea. John Lim, a lawyer and early leader of the Council of Korean Americans, says, "Korean Americans are uniquely positioned to influence the U.S. government. With CKA as a unified platform, Korean Americans could make a meaningful impact in the geopolitical landscape."[7]

The truth is, Korean Americans will be involved in Korea for years and decades to come and so will the United States, as peace and progress work their way. In the traditional way of immigrants' offspring and descendants, they will visit the land of their parents and grandparents, study its history, and explain it to their children even as they engage their families in issues of the United States and its evolving society.

From the start, this book takes Korean Americans as examples of people and nations from all over the world who have played their parts in building this, America, this "shining city on a hill," as Ronald Reagan put it. And the book chronicles the competitive spirit and hard work, the deep faith and strong commitment of Koreans over more than seven decades to achieve their American vision.

But seven decades is a short time for this new immigrant group to have come so far. So to sum up, the book asks, what qualities have enabled the Korean community to adapt relatively quickly and contribute to American life? Was it their competitiveness? Or their Confucian rigor honed by centuries of colonization and poverty? Or is it their sense of obligation and social commitment born of deep religious faith? Obviously it is all of those things plus one more. They have come to the United States even as America has been coming to a new understanding of its geography. Previous immigrants from Asia were often denied acceptance. Chinese people came to "Gold Mountain" in the 1850s only to see immigration of Chinese laborers curtailed by the Chinese Exclusion Act of 1882. Japanese-born immigrants could not be naturalized; even their U.S.-born children, who were citizens, were shamefully sent to internment camps during World War II. But Korean immigrants, for all their rude awakening in the 1992 Riots and some continued sullen resistance on the part of closed-minded Americans even today, have been able to educate their children and attain recognition and welcome—as have most Asian Americans today. Los Angeles and California and really all parts of the United States recognize that we are at home in the Pacific World. And the Korean community is a great presence and strong contributor to America's future.

I have been helped in my years of research for this book by scores of people and organizations in the United States and Korea. I'll mention a half dozen or so but thank you all for honoring me with your teaching as I hope this book honors you. Let me acknowledge Professor Je Hoon Lee of the Network of Korean American Leaders at the University of Southern California, John Lim and Sam Yoon of the Council of Korean Americans, Spencer Kim of the Pacific Century Institute, Hyepin Im of Faith and Community Empowerment, Jihee and Peter Huh of Pacific American Fish Co., Professor Edward Taehan Chang of the University of California, Riverside, and the Young Oak Kim Center, and Professor Richard Drobnick of the University of Southern California.

My thanks also go to the editors and peer reviewers at University of Nevada Press. Thanks posthumously to scholar and friend Kevin Starr. And thanks to my beloved wife, Patricia, and our family, who have endured years of talk and absentmindedness from the writer. God bless you all.

CHAPTER 1

Icon of the Korean Community for L.A.

The seventy-three-story Wilshire Grand Tower stands out in downtown Los Angeles, a landmark erected by Korean Airlines (KAL) and Hanjin Group at a cost of $1.3 billion. It is the tallest building west of Chicago. But Chairman Yang Ho Cho, head of Korean Air and Hanjin, calls the project much more than an emblem of his family companies. "This will be an icon of the Korean community for Los Angeles," he said eight years ago,[1] when he gave an initial approval for the building that was dedicated as Wilshire Grand Center in 2017.

In using "icon," a word that connotes a sacred image, Cho wanted to honor his fellow Koreans through his Wilshire Grand Center. He wanted it to serve as a symbol for them and their children to take pride in their success as immigrants. His thoughts, expressed in an interview, speak of immigrants "who came here and started businesses and learned trades." He talks of Los Angeles as a "microcosm of the United States—a land built of immigrants who want to do one thing: improve their lives."[2]

As this book tells of Korean American history, it will also tell of Los Angeles' emergence as capital of the Asia Pacific region, a new western perspective for the United States. In fits and starts, America's focus over the past century has shifted to Asia, from its making the Philippines a U.S. territory in 1898, to war with Japan, and then rebuilding Japan and freeing up Korea. Involvement in Asia continued with fighting in the Korean War, later fighting in Vietnam, and relations with rising China that have developed through several changes over the decades. Most important, America in the last fifty-plus years has been more welcoming to immigrants from Asian countries than ever before. Through it all, Korea—divided as it is—has become an interesting partner of the United States, a source of ambitious professionals and energetic entrepreneurs. It's a great story; let us go forward.

Korean immigrants have been part of America's pivot to Asia, as citizens of Asian background have risen to almost twenty million from under one million a half-century ago. That surge was made possible by the 1965 Immigration and Nationality Act, which reversed a century of restrictions and injustice toward Asian peoples. Korean Americans today, at more than 1.7 million across the United States,[3] are still a relatively small group compared to new Americans from China, the Philippines, and India. But with energy and drive, Korean Americans are building landmarks in New York as well as L.A., lobbying for causes in Washington, founding businesses, heading universities and hospitals, and holding public office in all parts of the United States. They are working for affordable housing and family services through more than seven thousand Korean churches across the country. In education Korean students, pushed by parents to excel, are cited by former U.S. Secretary of Education Arne Duncan, who asks why American kids can't be more like Koreans.

Word of caution: There are no "model minorities," and Korean Americans vehemently object to being seen as such. But tales of Koreans can reflect how all Americans—including Native Americans—came to be. It is not a matter of tribe or color or religious beliefs but of culture and opportunity. All peoples "become" Americans, as generations embrace new culture while cherishing the old. It is both a wonder and a mission.

Jihee Huh, a prominent Korean American woman who has won commendation from the U.S. Congress, sums up the Korean community this way: "We are a very eclectic people with many talents but most importantly focus on education and hard work as our collective mantra."[4] Her reference to education reflects the history of a class system in Korea that denied education to all but the aristocracy or Yangban class who could be educated and thus serve in government and the leading agencies of society. Indeed, in the Confucian social codes that ruled ancient Korea, women could not be taught to read and write in the official state language. Since Korea became an independent country at the end of World War II, its people have become fierce about education for their children.

Korea, a land with 2,000 years of recorded history, "was an ancient society of landlords and peasants, tightly bound to the aristocracy or Yangban class," says Edward Taehan Chang, professor of ethnic studies at the University of California Riverside.[5] "Education was restricted to the landowning class—and education was the only way to rise and succeed in society," the professor explains. Chang is director of the Young

Oak Kim Center at the university. He immigrated to the United States in 1974 and earned degrees in sociology and Asian American Studies at UC Berkeley and UCLA. Over more than two decades at UC Riverside, he has become a widely honored authority on the modern history of Korea, a peninsular country frequently threatened by larger neighbors China on the west and Japan to the east.

Like its neighbors, Korea severely limited contact with outsiders, whether foreign missionaries or adventurous European traders, through the seventeenth and eighteenth centuries and into the nineteenth. And few Koreans ventured forth upon the seas themselves. That's why explorers dubbed it the "hermit kingdom."[6] But since the late nineteenth century, Korea's people have begun to move to other countries, to China, Japan, and, importantly, the United States, where they first immigrated in 1903. Korean independence was lost in 1910,[7] when Japan formally colonized the country. Eventually during that colonization, Japan tried to ban the Korean language and force families to adopt a Japanese form of their Korean names—Kanemura rather than Kim, for example.

All of that came to an end with Japan's World War II defeat in 1945. Korea was then divided between the United States government, including military forces in South Korea and the Soviet Union in North Korea. Military forces from the Communist North attacked the South in June of 1950, beginning the Korean War, which lasted until a truce in 1953. It was the first military engagement of the Cold War. Armed forces of the United States, the Republic of Korea, and the United Nations fought troops from North Korea, which had become a satellite of the Soviet Union and an ally of Communist China. The U.S. military suffered 36,574 deaths in battle, with more than 100,000 wounded; South Korea lost 217,000 military and a total of 1 million of its people; North Korea lost 406,000 military and 600,000 of its people; and China lost 600,000 military.[8]

Chinese armed forces entered the conflict after the U.S. military under the command of Gen. Douglas MacArthur had pushed North Korean armies back near the Yalu River border with China in October 1950. The war then entered a phase of lingering combat until July 1953, when a truce—but not a peace treaty—ended fighting. The 600-mile-long Korean peninsula remains divided today between the Communist-led government of North Korea, 25 million in population, and the U.S.-allied Republic of Korea to the south, 50 million people. The United States continues to have 28,000 military stationed in South Korea.[9]

To Professor Chang the Korean War, cruel as it was, brought his native country into the modern world. "Korea was able to become a

Tower at Wilshire Grand Center, Los Angeles, tallest building in the West, completed 2017. Courtesy of Korean Air.

modern society with education the key to success in life," he says. "For the Korean immigrants, too, the name of the game was education for their children. They believed so strongly that they worked 17 hours a day in small grocery stores and garment factories to make money for their children's education."[10]

Tom Suh, for example, immigrated to Los Angeles in 1995. He set up a photography shop to earn a living, taking photos for passports and social occasions. Like immigrants have always done, he talks of struggles to adapt to a new country. "I don't speak so good the English. I work here 20 years and I have learned to read it but to speak English, I make mistakes. I could go to school, but I must keep open this shop every day," he says. But his tone and demeanor change when he turns to his family. "My daughters are smart. One is at UC Berkeley and another is at UC Irvine, and my youngest daughter is at BYU (Brigham Young University), in Provo, Utah," he says. "I am Mormon," Suh adds firmly. Suh remains a Korean immigrant in his mind, but he sees his daughters as Korean American.[11]

Thus, the Korean American population is composed partly of immigrants from colonial persecution and war-torn poverty, who struggled with language, isolation, and violence in their early years in America.

But increasingly the children and grandchildren of those immigrants are now claiming a place in the give-and-take of American society. So there's the picture: Korean Americans with their ambitions are telling anew the age-old story of immigration, of people who leave an old world behind and bring new energy and vision to America.

In concrete terms—pardon the pun—they have begun to build monuments. In New York, developer Young Woo,[12] who came from Korea by way of Argentina, is building a Super Pier on the Hudson River. The $350 million project will house offices and restaurants, health clubs and spas, and even a park on the roof of a rebuilt old pier that once welcomed ocean liners. It will be completed in 2019.

The largest monument of course is the Wilshire Grand Center, which Yang Ho Cho thought about building in Los Angeles over most of the 1980s. "The Wilshire Grand is designed to enhance Los Angeles' standing as the capital of the Pacific Rim," Cho says. "While we originally designed the project as two freestanding towers, we came to the conclusion from both aesthetic and economic standpoints that one beautiful tower would make the impact we desired and produce a positive return on our investment."[13]

"Capital of the Pacific Rim" and "Gateway to the Pacific" are new descriptions for the city of Los Angeles, a growing recognition that the region always seen as "the West Coast" might as accurately be seen as the eastern coast of a vast Pacific world. It is but one more perspective for Los Angeles, a metropolis less than 250 years old from the day Felipe de Neve, governor of Spanish California, named the settlement El Pueblo Sobre El Río de Nuestra Senora La Reina de Los Angeles de Porciuncola—the last word in a long official name referring to a Franciscan chapel in Italy.[14] The region was inhabited by Chumash, Tongva, and Gabrielino natives for millennia before priests and soldiers from the Spanish Empire came north from Mexico to build missions and name cities. They ventured from San Diego to Santa Ana; San Gabriel to Santa Monica; and on up the coast to Santa Barbara, San Jose, and San Francisco. Ranchero landowners named Sepulveda and Domínguez raised cattle and horses, but then gave way to other settlers who discovered oil in Los Angeles and Long Beach along with the remains of prehistoric mastodons in La Brea.

Los Angeles blossomed in the twentieth century as sons and daughters of immigrants from Russia, Poland, and Germany named Mayer and Loew, Warner and Laemmle, Fox and Goldwyn made it the capital of the movie industry, which took on the name Hollywood. And visionaries from everywhere in America and abroad followed through to make the Los Angeles region a center of the world.

So we come to Yang Ho Cho's story in the forty-four years he has divided his time between L.A. and Seoul.[15] When he came to Los Angeles in 1974 to manage the U.S. operations of Korean Air, the company had just expanded its transpacific service with a Boeing 747—the first airline to do so. Y. H., the eldest son of Cho Choong Hoon, founder of Hanjin, was twenty-five at the time. His father's company had served the American armed forces before, during, and after the Korean War. Cho Choong Hoon was close to the government of Syngman Rhee, first president of the Republic of Korea. And he was then close to Park Chung Hee, who took over as president in 1961 and began a determined program of economic development. Park entrusted Korean Air Lines, the government company, to Cho Choong Hoon in 1969.

A note on names: Korean names in Korea are stated with surname first. Those in this book will be given in the format [surname, given name]. Koreans in America follow the U.S. custom of given name and then surname last. This book follows the American pattern for all Korean residents of the United States and of course Korean American citizens.

Cho's and Other Korean American Businesses

Yang Ho Cho, had first come to America when his father sent him to prep school at Cushing Academy in Ashburnham, Massachusetts. He then earned a degree in industrial engineering at Inha University, in Inchon, Korea, which had been founded in 1954 as a technological research institute by Syngman Rhee.

But when Y. H. came to Los Angeles in 1974, he did not run his operation simply as a visiting executive for a foreign airline. He integrated himself into the society of L.A. He joined the first class of the University of Southern California's International Business Education and Research program, which was founded in 1978 to train working executives from around the world in one-year MBA programs. Cho earned his MBA in 1979, but that year was only the first of a long association with the university. Cho's sister and two brothers attended USC as have his son and two daughters. Cho calls Los Angeles his "second home"; "USC has changed lives both in Korea and America," he says. Cho and his family have endowed scholarships for young Korean American students at USC and supported development of a Korean Heritage Library at the university. Cho himself became a trustee of USC in 1997.

The University of California Los Angeles (UCLA) also has become a big draw for Asian students. Both schools are now teaching classes in China, Korea, Singapore, and other countries—underlining Los Angeles's connections to the Pacific Rim. There are tensions at present due to shifting policies of the new U.S. administration, which sow fear and confusion overseas.

Over four decades, Cho has engineered the growth of Korean Air, as travel from Asia has greatly expanded. He has been forward thinking in many ways. In 1989, for example, Korean Air and Hanjin bought the old Statler Hotel, built in 1952 as a landmark for young and burgeoning Los Angeles.[16] At a Statler dedication ceremony that year, California governor Earl Warren and L.A. mayor Fletcher Bowron presided while film actor and emcee Ronald Reagan introduced the glittering crowd. The hotel was renamed the Wilshire Grand in 1999. A decade later, as the building neared its sixtieth birthday, Cho had to make decisions about renovating or rebuilding it. He chose first to rebuild it as two structures: a 560-room luxury hotel and a sixty-five-story office building. But he changed his mind in 2011 and committed to building the seventy-three-story glass-and-steel monument that holds an Intercontinental Hotel of 900 rooms plus twenty floors of offices and another ten stories of shops, restaurants, and ballrooms.

The 1980s were an outward-looking time for Los Angeles as Japanese auto companies Nissan, Honda, and Toyota based their U.S. headquarters there while they opened manufacturing centers in Tennessee, Ohio, and Kentucky. Korea's Hyundai Motor Company set up an American operation in Garden Grove in Orange County in 1986 and was immediately successful for a short time before suffering setbacks. Hyundai made a comeback in the early 2000s and has since grown into a major carmaker in the United States. Korean Air began flying two flights a day between LAX and Asia, and Hanjin expanded operations at the port of Long Beach, as foreign trade grew through the ports of L.A. and Long Beach. The two cities have become America's largest seaports.

But the world was changing dramatically. The Berlin Wall came down in 1989, and the massive Union of Soviet Socialist Republics (USSR) broke up in 1991. The effect on Los Angeles and all of Southern California was a deep and painful recession. Half a million jobs disappeared as the Defense Department cut back contracts.[17] Defense industry corporate headquarters shrank or merged out of existence.

The Korean community suffered a bitter blow and a wakeup call simultaneously in the Los Angeles riots of 1992, when both the police

Yang Ho Cho, chairman and CEO, Korean Air, called the Wilshire Tower the "icon of Korean Community for Los Angeles." Courtesy of Korean Air.

and L.A.'s political leadership ignored attacks on Koreans and their property. (The riots and their aftermath are covered in chapter 4.) Paradoxically, however, Asian communities seemed to prosper in this era. Four economies of Asia—Hong Kong, South Korea, Taiwan, and Singapore—grew rapidly and became known as the "Four Tigers." In the New York area, Korean communities settled in the borough of Queens—an area called Flushing, named after Dutch settlers who founded the city centuries ago—and near midtown Manhattan. More than 800,000 Koreans and Korean Americans live in that region today.

Korean immigrants lived in many communities in Southern California, but a concentration of some 7,000 settled in a mid-Wilshire neighborhood that became known as Koreatown. It became a center of Korean barbecue restaurants, bars and tea shops, stores and meeting rooms. Koreatown also is where the immigrants held an annual Korean Festival beginning in 1974, with a parade on Olympic Boulevard, just as immigrants in earlier ages held parades in cities across the United States. The Forty-Fourth Korean Festival parade, now a much larger event graced by mayors of local cities, including Los Angeles, stepped off in September 2017.

Koreatown also became the heart of political organizing for the community. The Korean American Coalition was formed there in 1983 to represent Korean concerns for civil rights and community development. Its stated mission was to establish channels of communication with elected officials, other community organizations, media, and the general public. In short, the mission was to speak up and tell the politicians and officials who run things in Los Angeles to recognize the Korean community.

"People are tired of not being heard at the level of the City Council," said Grace Yoo, who served five years as executive director of the coalition.[18] "We are small in numbers but we can have influence where people run the politics." Yoo, who came to the United States at age three with her parents, has won awards for her work with that coalition. She was raised in Glendale, graduated in political science from UC Riverside, and earned a law degree from New Jersey's Seton Hall University. In her years with the Korean American Coalition, she helped bring a Los Angeles Police Department station to Koreatown to protect the residents and shopkeepers. She also created programs to help high school students and to bring help to families in South Korea who are separated from relatives in North Korea. In 2015, Yoo ran for a seat on the Los Angeles City Council and lost. But she plans to run again for that seat in 2019 and has a better chance.

She has a law office on Wilshire Boulevard today and is involved in fighting for affordable housing to be included in new and remodeled buildings that are thriving now with residential development. While many areas of Los Angeles acquire a new luster, Yoo sees a need for new programs to help basic working families hurt by shrinking mass production in the city's garment industry and other changes affecting the restaurant and food industries. "I will run for office," Yoo declares, "because I'm fed up with the inability to do what is right for average citizens who are struggling to afford basic healthcare and make the rent in a tough changing economy."

Still, when asked why the Korean community should be seen as a beacon for the future, Yoo has a ready answer: "Fighting spirit!" she says, and explains, "When a terribly poor nation, that has been kicked around by neighbors over long history, rises to eleventh place in gross national product in the world, it indicates a smart, hardworking people who show what they can accomplish and teach the world."

Bold words but credible enough, considering examples in L.A.'s recent history in commercial real estate. Because Los Angeles suffered such a sharp recession in the early 1990s, it became a place where Korean immigrants could pool resources and acquire office buildings—an opportunity that did not exist in other cities. As the post–Cold War recession dragged on in the 1990s, insurance companies owning office buildings that were losing tenants gave up and sold Wilshire Boulevard structures at bargain prices. Korean investors stepped in to buy. Most prominent among them, Dr. David Lee,[19] an immigrant from Korea who had graduated in internal medicine from Northwestern University Medical School, got together with eight other Korean doctors and dentists to buy a Wilshire Boulevard building in 1995 for $6 million. A decade later, the building was worth five times that much and Dr. Lee and his Korean associates, who by then numbered over 100 in the Jamison Properties company, owned 70 office buildings, 13 medical buildings, and 6 shopping centers and ranked as the largest commercial property owners in Los Angeles County.

Who financed all that property buying? An Asian method of financing called *keh* in Korean, *hui* in Chinese and Vietnamese, and *tanomoshi* in Japanese financed it. In a keh, a dozen or so members in a group pool their money in monthly contributions and offer a sum one at a time to a member to start or expand a business or for some other purpose. The designated borrower offers an annual return to fellow members and pays back the investment in a matter of years, depending on whether the venture is successful. In Dr. Lee's case, he promised a 15 percent annual return to his partners, and he achieved that as real estate values appreciated in the late nineties. He credited Jamison's success at that time to long-term vision: "We invest on a six- to seven-year cycle while most investors are on three to five years," Lee said. Also, however, he increased cash flow for the investors by cutting back on upkeep of the buildings—minimal painting, cleaning, landscaping, and decor.

Moreover, the Wilshire Boulevard buildings gained new tenants as South Korea's advancing economy restructured some large companies and reduced staff. That caused an influx of Korean immigrants to Los Angeles and other areas. Not all were poor, laid-off employees either. Executives of large conglomerate or *chaebol* companies were forced into "early" retirement but with ample severance packages to augment their savings. As many already had children studying at U.S. universities, the executives moved to L.A. and began new ventures, renting offices and business premises with cash. Sure there were ups and downs. The low maintenance caught up with Jamison over the years, as corporate tenants protested and fought to break leases. Still Jamison remains a large company today, and Dr. Lee, helped by his daughter Jaime and son Garret, is converting office space to residential uses, creating apartment complexes out of office buildings, and converting some industrial and retail spaces in downtown L.A. "I follow money," the doctor said recently. "We need more apartments. If you create residential space, you can get double the rent as compared to office."

Daughter Jaime Lee, a graduate of USC and its Gould School of Law, has served as commissioner of Los Angeles's Industrial Development Authority. She describes a new vision of Koreatown and Los Angeles at large, as mass transit becomes a reality in the area renowned for worship of the automobile. "Koreatown is center city with great transit and parking," Jaime Lee says. "And residential conversions are part of an organic growth process for our company." She is also overseeing conversion of apparel industry showrooms to trendy workplaces for digital technology and media industries.

Y. H. Cho also made moves in the nineties as a trustee at USC, where he became a friend of a thirty-nine-year-old engineering professor named Chrysostomos L. "Max" Nikias, who came to USC in 1991 from the State University of New York at Buffalo.[20] Nikias, born in Cyprus, graduated in engineering from the National Technical University of Athens in 1977 and immigrated to Buffalo, where he earned a doctorate in electrical and mechanical engineering at SUNY Buffalo in 1982 and went on to become a member of the faculty of that school. After he came to USC, Cho and Nikias worked together to advance research programs in engineering and aerospace as Nikias rose to dean of engineering, then provost of the university, and ultimately in 2010 to become the eleventh president of the 138-year-old University of Southern California. Nikias also played a key role in Cho's decision to build the Wilshire Grand Tower as an architecturally significant structure.

Both Cho and Nikias speak proudly of their collaborations. "We have organized alliances such as the Aerospace Institute for Engineering Research, the Pratt & Whitney Institute for Collaborative Engineering, and the Korea Air/General Electric Research Institute for International Collaboration," Cho says.[21] The business connections are clear, of course. Korean Air is a major customer of both Pratt & Whitney and General Electric, the largest suppliers of aircraft engines worldwide.

Nikias talks expansively of "our plan to capitalize on our uniquely international heritage so that USC can emerge as a truly global university—one with students prepared for world citizenship and with faculty members who can cross academic and geographic boundaries in order to innovate,"[22] to which Cho adds, "I'm proud to have helped advance research because this has attracted more students from Asian countries and from Korea specifically."[23]

Such visions are splendid to be sure, but fulfilling them can be difficult. To build Korean Air into a leading international carrier and the busiest Asian airline serving LAX, Cho had to deal with a severe problem stemming from Korea's hierarchical Confucian culture. In the culture derived from the teachings of the Chinese scholar K'ung Fu-tzu, or Confucius, dating back twenty-six hundred years, sons and everyone else in the family are subject to fathers. Likewise, in business, employees are not only subject to managers, but they must show strict deference. Young people must bow before their elders. Specifically in an airliner's cockpit, junior officers never speak up to contradict a captain, even in a life-or-death situation. From the seventies through the nineties, Korean Air compiled a record of plane crashes and pilot errors that threatened to ground the airline. A crash in Guam in 1997, in which a KAL flight engineer failed to correct a captain's incorrect assumption that he could make a visual landing in heavy rain, caused the death of 228 passengers and crew and led to alarm over Korean flying. Then, another incident in 1999 occurred on a flight in Britain in which the Korean Air captain banked a jet out of control due to a faulty altitude indicator, even though his first officer was reading a correct indicator but failed to speak up to correct his superior officer.[24] After that incident, the U.S. Army forbade its personnel to fly with Korean Air; Delta Airlines and Air France suspended their flying partnership with Korean Air; and the Federal Aviation Administration and Canada's comparable agency considered revoking the airline's privileges. These measures forced Y. H. Cho to take direct action. He called on assistance from Delta and a Delta executive named David Greenberg, who developed new training programs for the airline's personnel, including a requirement that they learn to operate in the English language because that is the language of aviation worldwide. "If you are trying to land at JFK in rush hour, the tower is talking to you in English and you had better understand what is being said," Greenberg explained.[25]

Thanks to Cho's actions, KAL's people have adapted to the independent-thinking policies of international air transport, and Korean Air has had a superior safety record since that time. But note well, Cho did not ask his Delta instructors to lecture Korean Air people on their culture, recognizing that culture is a complex and cherished concept for all people—particularly immigrants who have adapted to new lands. Brian Lee, a lawyer and entrepreneur who has founded three successful companies in Los Angeles, refers to the "beauty and legacy of Our Korean Culture."[26]

Asked about Korean culture, Y. H. Cho gives a thoughtful if indirect answer. "The Korean culture is beautiful in tradition, but complex in composition," he says. "We are influenced by a variety of tenets of Christianity and Buddhism, and our culture has evolved from a history of refinement, occupation, freedom and growth. On one hand we have a rich tradition that we try to respect, and on the other we have a current culture that might question respect. Because of this, Korean culture is becoming far less formal and perhaps a little less reverent of its past."[27]

Turmoil and Change in the Homeland

It should be noted that much of the time that Korean immigrants were building new lives in Los Angeles and the United States, the Republic of Korea was in fairly constant political turmoil. General Park Chung-hee, a military leader, took over the Republic's government in a coup in 1961. (He was the father of the recently impeached president Park Geun-hye.) Park Chung-hee launched a long-term policy of economic growth by setting up industrial training for young Koreans, sending immigrants to South America and ultimately to the United States, and supporting the rise of large corporations, or *chaebol*, to build up modern industry.[28] Young Koreans were sent to mine coal in Germany and in the 1970s to serve as construction crews to build new cities in Saudi Arabia, which had become flush with capital after the price of oil rose dramatically.

Meanwhile South Korea engaged in the political equivalent of civil war. Park's agents, known as the Korean CIA (KCIA), kidnapped political foe and future president Kim Dae Jung in 1973 and were going to kill him, but President Jimmy Carter intervened to stop the killing. Park himself was assassinated by the head of KCIA over dinner one night in 1979. Turmoil continued off and on for the next two decades, until Kim Dae Jung won the presidency in 1997 in the first peaceful election. Kim then launched a program to reform the chaebol and engaged in political and legal battles with Hanjin founder Cho Choong Hoon and with Y. H. Cho also. Indeed, President Kim blamed Korean Air's crashes in the preceding years on the fact that the airline was part of the Hanjin conglomerate.[29] "Instead of making the best efforts to acquire skilled pilots," he said, "the owners concentrate too much on profits." As things turned out, Kim's administration brought tax evasion charges against both Cho Choong Hoon and Y. H. Cho. But the elder Cho was by that time in ill health, and the government declined to prosecute him. Instead they brought charges against Y. H. Cho, who was forced to resign as head of Korean Air temporarily and even serve time in jail. However, Cho Choong Hoon died in 2002 at age eighty-two, and his son Y. H. was appointed to lead the whole Hanjin Group and Korean Air in 2003.

What really was going on in the politics of Korea at that time was a reaction: The giant conglomerate companies—names like Samsung, Hyundai, Hanjin, and others—had been given mandates starting in the sixties to expand everywhere with little or no regulation or oversight. Inevitably, political opposition and resentments rose up over time and reforms were introduced and compromises made. South Korea's economic rise has continued: A relatively small country, the Republic of Korea is now the eleventh-largest economy in the world, ahead of Russia, Australia, Spain, Iran, Saudi Arabia, and many others.[30] A similar reaction against chaebol wealth and political influence was behind the impeachment of President Park Geun-hye in 2016–2017.

The Cho family has played a major role in Korea's rise. Y. H. spoke of his father's accomplishments more than a decade ago. Cho Choong Hoon, he said, "transformed Korea's stature internationally and created cultural and business opportunities for Koreans."[31] A driving force in modern Korean industry, Choong Hoon started Hanjin with a single truck in 1945 and soon put his transportation equipment at the service of the U.S. military before and during the Korean War. In that early postcolonial decade, U.S. military operations and investments were the only economic forces sustaining a new nation of small farms and towns. Many industrious young Koreans got their start providing services to U.S. Army bases. Cho Choong Hoon's Hanjin was particularly successful and farsighted.

Then, when the U.S. military entered the Vietnam War, with some support services from the Republic of Korea's personnel, Cho's Hanjin expanded into ocean shipping to transport supplies to the military in Vietnam and build ports for the U.S. Navy. Later Cho pioneered containerized freight shipping for Korea. Hanjin, which had been early to lease terminal space in Long Beach, California, made South Korea the number 2 shipper into that port and number 3 shipper into the port of Los Angeles at San Pedro. China is number 1 in both ports and Japan number 2 in the L.A. port.

However, some parts of the current company have run into problems. Hanjin Shipping came upon hard times starting in 2007, as the U.S. and worldwide recession slowed freight shipments. As the slowdown dragged on, Korean Air, which was doing better than the shipper, raised more than $3 billion in 2013–2014 by selling assets and used the money to settle Hanjin's debts. Yet matters became very much worse in 2015–2016, as China's economy slowed international shipping even further. In August 2016 Hanjin Shipping filed for bankruptcy protection. Yet this caused another crisis as Hanjin ships, filled with cargo, could not enter ports to unload because the bankrupt company could not pay fees to terminals. Cargo containers worth some $14 billion remained stranded aboard ships.[32]

Relief came in September 2016 when the parent company, Hanjin Group, pledged $60 million to pay the necessary fees, and Yang Ho Cho himself stepped up with $40 million of his personal funds to help. The names of both Korean Air and Hanjin are on the Wilshire Grand Center, which has been developing since 2013 at Figueroa Street and Wilshire Boulevard in downtown Los Angeles.

The building holds another distinction: It is the first tall structure completed in Los Angeles in twenty-five years or since the post–Cold War downturn caused a recession. Also, economic growth was not supportive of traditional office buildings in Southern California for years before that, as the local economy shifted from big banks and buildings downtown to new technology industries in Santa Monica, Venice, El Segundo, and other coastal cities near the airport, as well as Pasadena, near the California Institute of Technology, and Orange County to the south. Foreign trade, as the ports of L.A. and Long Beach grew to take in 40 percent of all goods entering the United States, also gave rise to an expanding logistics industry in smaller cities in L.A. and San Bernardino Counties.[33]

Now downtown Los Angeles is becoming residential with a growing arts district and old buildings being converted to modern designer workplaces. That is one reason why the Wilshire Grand Center with its tower is composed of fifty-three stories of hotel, shops, and restaurants and twenty stories of office space. When Y. H. Cho authorized the Wilshire Grand project in 2012, he was looking ahead to a "new Renaissance for Los Angeles," says Christopher Martin, chairman of A.C. Martin Partners, a company that had helped to build Los Angeles City Hall in 1927–1928 and that has served as project manager and architect of the Wilshire Grand.[34]

Martin recalls a renaissance timeline for the city from the "early 1900s, when Los Angeles was the regional shopping center for California, to the 1930s, when it became Oil Town USA as Standard Oil of California (now

Chevron), Superior Oil, Atlantic Richfield, and Signal Oil put up office buildings in downtown L.A. Then corporate headquarters followed and banks and financial institutions—Union Bank, Security Pacific, Bank of America—made L.A. the financial capital of the western U.S. Then in 1992, everything changed," Martin says.

"Banks moved up to San Francisco or merged out of state," he goes on. "We had a long layover as office towers emptied out and smaller companies, professional offices, and nonprofit organizations occupied buildings at lower, more affordable leases. And then, at the turn of the millennium, Staples Arena and the L.A. Live complex brought sports and entertainment to downtown, and buildings converted to residential housing. L.A. started to become a twenty-four-hour city with people pushing baby carriages. And about 2004 Y. H. Cho, who loves L.A., thought about making an investment to turn the old Statler-cum-Wilshire hostelry into a four-star hotel on an international scale."

It was at that time that Martin, a USC graduate himself, first met Yang Ho Cho. "Our firm was doing work at the USC engineering school, and Max Nikias suggested I meet with Y. H. Cho who owns Korean Air," Martin recalls. "So we had dinner, and he asked me to look at property he owns on Jeju Island off Korea." One thing led to another, and Martin invited Cho to visit a ranch his family owns near Yosemite National Park. Yosemite captivated Cho so much that the curved glass top of the Wilshire Grand building today is meant to reflect the shape of Half Dome, the park's distinctive rock formation.

More pertinent to the new Wilshire Grand, Cho later requested that the A.C. Martin firm supply the architectural design. David Martin, A.C. Martin's chief architect and a cousin of Christopher, was at work on design as permits were approved in 2010. The final launch of the project, Chris Martin recalls, came about when "Governor (Arnold) Schwarzenegger called Gary Toebben, head of the L.A. Chamber of Commerce, and said he was going to Asia and wanted to announce a deal for California with Korea." Martin set up a breakfast meeting between Y. H. Cho and Schwarzenegger. Cho told the governor, "If you come to Korea, I will host an event and announce that I will build this project." Cho announced the project in Korea and later in L.A. He then turned the big job of project management over to the A.C. Martin company.

His model, Martin says, "is Rockefeller Center in New York, which was built during the 1930s Great Depression by a visionary family who ordered the highest quality. Cho's aim was that his Korean family would give Los Angeles a landmark building of great quality, as the Rockefeller family had given New York. Thus Cho ordered that the Wilshire Grand was to be done with the finest-quality materials."

The shining glass tower now stands resplendent, its ascension rising seventy-three stories. Note that over the three years of construction, the Wilshire Grand has set records and precedents for building in Los Angeles and elsewhere. Obviously before you construct a seventy-three-story edifice you must set a foundation, and the tower's builders did so in February 2014 in what is called "The Big Pour." After a pit 18 feet deep had been cleared and seven million pounds of reinforcing steel had been inserted into the space, the USC Marching Band serenaded Y. H. Cho, architect David Martin, L.A. Mayor Eric Garcetti, and others who made speeches. Then eighty-four million pounds of concrete were poured constantly through eighteen hours from 5 p.m. Saturday February 15 to Sunday morning February 16, 2014. Speed was of the essence as the concrete had to solidify on a precise schedule, more fresh stuff coming in before the previous load had hardened. The Guinness Book of Records was there to record this biggest, fastest pour ever.

The building has a special firefighters' vestibule, staircase, and elevator. Conceiving of and designing a supertall building in the post-9/11 age demanded that the builders think about New York's World Trade Center and the terrible dilemma of people on upper floors whom firefighters could not reach. They were forced to choose to die in the flames or by leaping out to certain death in midair. So the first section that was built in the Wilshire Grand is the central concrete core that holds elevators and stairwells. "We put in extra staircases and an elevator that enables firefighters to go from underground levels to the top of the building," says Chris Martin.

That central core makes the Wilshire Grand different from other tall buildings in the city. Previously all tall buildings had to have helicopter pads on top so that firefighters could rescue people from burning premises. Doing away with the necessity of a helicopter pad allows the Wilshire Grand to have the curved glass Half Dome replica as its signature top, not to mention a terrace and swimming pool on the seventy-third floor. The circular red and white symbol of the South Korean flag glows brightly on that curved glass top today.

For Los Angeles, the Wilshire Grand's timing was a step ahead of a growing field. Soon after the Korean Air project was announced, Greenland Development, a Shanghai-based company, announced a four-building project at Eighth Street near the Harbor Freeway called Metropolis. It will be completed in 2018 and feature office buildings and condominiums that are now being sold as vacation opportunities to newly wealthy customers in China. Downtown L.A. has blossomed with new projects. New hotels and apartment buildings are going up along the Figueroa Corridor facing L.A. Live, Staples Arena, and the Convention Center. And farther down Figueroa Street, the massive University Village project of usc has built $650 million in academic space, and housing for faculty and for twenty-five hundred undergraduates, plus retail and restaurant premises in a single community that is part of the main campus.

There is an excitement among real estate people who see money flowing into L.A. from China, Asia, and other areas of the world. They see the Wilshire Grand and other projects as auspicious signals of a new day. Chris Martin says, "L.A. is bursting forth, a new world city. That is why I wanted Wilshire Grand to be the poster child for international investment, saying to the world come to Los Angeles, *this* is the place to be."[35]

Some leaders of the local economy pay tribute to the man who built the new landmark. Bill Allen, president of the Los Angeles County Economic Development Corp., says, "No one has been more important to building a relationship between Korea and Southern California than Chairman Y. H. Cho."[36]

And Y. H. himself has spoken about the building several times as it was going up. In an interview for this book he said: "I believe in the future of Los Angeles and want to be an integral part of its success. Los Angeles deserves to be the capital of the Pacific Rim considering its location and attractions." He added that "the transpacific corridor is going to get busier and grow with the success of South America and Asia. The role of lax as a hub will only increase with the free trade agreement between the U.S. and Korea." Then in a different vein, Y. H., who dedicated the tower on his sixty-seventh birthday in 2017, waxed sentimental: "Keep in mind," he said in an interview, "we are not only developing the largest building west of the Mississippi; we are creating an iconic image for my adopted home. L.A. has been my second home for more than forty years! So the project is important for me personally."[37]

"Capital of the Pacific Rim," the phrase Y. H. Cho and others use referring to Los Angeles lately, is not mere business jargon, says David Zuercher, a now-retired executive who led international operations for Wells Fargo & Co.[38] "Only in Los Angeles do all the cultures of the Pacific meet," he notes. "In communities from China, Japan, Korea, Philippines, Vietnam, India, and Southeast Asia as well as Australia and Mexico and South America. Los Angeles is unique." Read on. This book on Korean Americans will highlight this idea of America's understanding of itself as a family member of the Pacific World, a focus different from that of the eastern United States and its Atlantic mindset.

Finally, what of the Korean community to whom Cho dedicated the building? There is a pride among young Korean Americans seeing the landmark display Korean ownership and success. But it is a quiet pride, as one might compliment a historic statue. Marilyn Flynn, dean of the USC School of Social Work since 1997 and a scholar who lived in Korea and attracted Korean scholars to the school, has a more textured view. When she was helping to found the Network of Korean American Leaders in 2005 as part of USC's Asian Pacific Center, government officials and experts from Korea came to talk to students and bring lessons from the old country. But the lectures did not go over well.[39]

"The students were polite but thought that many of the old country's lessons did not really work for them," says Professor Flynn. "They were living here and had to find their own way in this new country." Her implication is unstated but clear, a reference to a tradition as old as Plymouth Colony and Roanoke Island, as the immigration stations of Ellis Island in New York Harbor and Angel Island in San Francisco Bay: As offspring and descendants of immigrants from every part of the world have ever done, the Koreans of L.A. and the United States are adapting to American culture while adding the "beauty and legacy" of their Korean culture to strengthen the mix. This book is a story of that.

Yet who were the Korean community's founders in America, who are its leaders today, and where do this new American community and those who have been here longer hope to be tomorrow? The next chapter will start to explore these questions.

CHAPTER 2

Pioneers, Heroes, and Law
That Made Asian America

The Korean community has a longer history in Los Angeles than is often recognized. The first Korean residents came in the late 1800s as diplomats, merchants and other travelers. In late 1902–early 1903 some 102 Koreans, many of them professionals and teachers, voyaged aboard the *SS Gaelic* to Hawaii and then on to San Francisco with intentions to remain in California and work to help their Korean homeland from these shores. A century later, in 2003, those pioneers were officially celebrated by U.S. president George W. Bush, who declared January 13 every year as Korean American Day.[1]

They were followed in greater numbers in 1907, when seven thousand Korean men arrived in Hawaii to work on sugarcane plantations. Hawaii wouldn't be a state for another half century, but it was a temporary home for many of those men, for they were allowed to bring in "picture brides." In Hawaii they were hearing plenty about California, a better place to be, and many who subsequently made their way to the mainland with those brides became the bedrock of today's century-long Korean community. Their main bases, then as now, were Los Angeles and Riverside Counties.

America's Koreans faced every hardship that all waves of immigrants had to cope with—the distrust and ignorance that belittled and tested the various nationalities and ethnicities that have come together as the U.S. fabric.

Let's look at stories of two men who illustrate their struggles and their passions. First, Dosan Ahn Chang Ho,[2] a man who led the fight for Korean independence from Japan's colonial rule, and second, Young Oak Kim,[3] who became an American hero in World War II and the Korean War and then a community leader in civilian life.

Dosan Ahn Chang Ho's name is on a sign at the interchange of the Harbor 110 and Santa Monica 10 Freeways near downtown Los

Angeles. Most people driving by might guess that the name is Korean but wouldn't know anything else. Ahn was his last name. In American usage, he would be Chang Ho Ahn. (The word Dosan means "island mountain," and Ahn took it as a pen name after seeing the peak in Hawaii on his first voyage to America in 1902.) The name also adorns many other places and monuments in the L.A. area: the Ahn Chang Ho post office in Los Angeles, the Ahn Chang Ho memorial statue in Riverside, Ahn Chang Ho Square at Jefferson Boulevard and Van Buren Place, the highway interchange downtown, and the Ahn family home on Thirty-Fourth Street in Los Angeles that is now on the USC campus and houses the Korean Studies Institute.

By any measure, Ahn Chang Ho is worthy of U.S. history books, for he is an immigrant to Los Angeles who became a renowned leader of Korean efforts to gain independence from Japan in the first years of the twentieth century. In the turmoil immediately before and during the Japanese occupation of Korea, he called for the moral and spiritual renewal of the Korean people through education.

Ahn and his wife—Hye-ryeon Lee, or Helen—came to San Francisco in 1902, the first Korean couple to immigrate to America. At twenty-four years of age, Ahn enrolled in an American elementary school in order to learn English and to study the American school system. He went on to found schools wherever he settled in the United States as well as back in Korea and in other areas of Korean emigration in Asia. According to *Dosan: The Man and His Thought*, a book that contains reports and reflections from many Korean writers and thinkers, Ahn worked hard to encourage his fellow Koreans to adapt to their new country. In San Francisco he would visit immigrant homes and instruct the people in ways to become more American in dress and demeanor. For all his scholarship and authority, he appears to have had the common touch: "He put up curtains, cleaned their houses and planted flowers in the gardens," according to one account.

The Ahns then moved to Riverside, where he organized the Korean Labor Movement in the citrus groves and other worksites. "To pick even one orange with sincerity in an American orchard will make a contribution to our country," Ahn Chang Ho is remembered for preaching.[4] In 1914 the family moved to Los Angeles, where their home became a way station for Koreans entering the United States and an important gathering place for the independence movement. Helen Ahn worked various domestic jobs to support the family and also provided financial support to help her husband when he was away from home—which was often for long periods. With five children to rear by herself—three boys and two girls—she worked hard.

In March 1919, the Korean Independence Movement became extremely active. Ahn and Syngman Rhee traveled to China and set up a Korean government in exile in Shanghai. Appointed premier, Ahn held the post until 1921. (Rhee would become the first president of the Republic of Korea in 1948.) The Shanghai effort was no small endeavor. It organized a full international Korean independence effort, very much including a movement in California that saw the founding of an aviation school in 1920 at Willows, a town north of Sacramento. Young Korean American student pilots who had been training at the Redwood City Aviation School formed the first cadre of fliers at Willows.[5] Formally named the Korean Aviation School, the academy was dedicated in July 1920. The school had great support from Korean rice farmers in its northern California region, and trained sixteen pilots during its brief existence. However, floods in the region took their toll on the rice farmers' prosperity in 1921, and the Willows school closed in June of that year. But its tradition continued in the Korean community, leading to Korean American pilots flying for the U.S. forces against Japan in World War II and forming the nucleus of the Republic of Korea's air force when independence came.

Meanwhile, Ahn Chang Ho returned home to Los Angeles in the early 1920s but left again in 1926 to go to Korea and China to work for independence. He was arrested and released several times by the Japanese rulers, serving four years in prison beginning in 1932. Then at the outset of Japan's war of conquest in China, Ahn was arrested in 1937, sent to prison again and tortured, but released to a hospital because he was suffering from tuberculosis. He died in the hospital on March 10, 1938, at age fifty-nine.

Physicians at the Gyeongsang University Hospital later recounted some of Ahn's statements to the Japanese police, according to the *Dosan* book. When they asked Ahn if he would give up his independence struggle, he replied that he could not. "When I eat, I eat for Korean independence. This will not change as long as I live," he said.[6] But Ahn spoke in a nuanced way about colonization and independence, the book reports. "I don't want to see Japan perish," he said. "Rather I want to see Japan become a good nation. Infringing upon Korea, your neighbor, will never prove profitable to you. Japan will profit by having 30 million Koreans as her friendly neighbors and not by annexing 30 million spiteful people," he is reported to have told his interrogators. "Therefore, to assert Korean independence is tantamount to desiring the well-being of Japan." To be sure, that sounds noble—but it also sounds smart.

The family Ahn left behind in Los Angeles made its mark in several ways. Son Philip Ahn has a star on Hollywood's Walk of Fame because he succeeded in playing villainous Japanese officers in the war films of the 1940s. He later started a popular restaurant in Panorama City. Soorah Ahn, the younger of two daughters, also acted and played in an episode of *M.A.S.H.* (Mobile Army Surgical Hospital) in 1977 alongside Alan Alda. The successful movie and then TV show, depicting stories from the Korean War, was filmed and taped in Malibu Creek State Park up near Mulholland Drive.

Best known of the family, Susan Ahn Cuddy enlisted in 1942 and became the first Asian American woman to serve in the U.S. Navy.[7] She then rose to gunnery officer, training men to fight the air war in the Pacific. Later, during the Cold War, Susan worked in intelligence for the National Security Agency leading three hundred agents in the Russia section.

Susan Ahn Cuddy was truly an extraordinary figure, who lived to be 100 years old before passing in 2015. She retired from the military in 1959 and became a much honored advocate of justice for Asian Americans and women's rights. She spoke often of her early years and of her mother, Helen, who was a leader of the Patriotic Organization of Korean American Women in 1936. "My mother, like many of the women, were left behind as their husbands went to work for Korean independence," Susan said in videos made later in her life. Her own father, she said, "allowed us to grow up rough, we did not need to be 'ladylike.' I played baseball because my mother said it was good to play an American sport."[8]

Her father, Ahn Chang Ho, left the family in California for the last time as he went to work for Korean independence in 1926. "It was hard knowing that you didn't have a country," she recalled. "There was a grocer on the corner in our neighborhood and he was Jewish and said that he did not have a homeland either. He helped us a lot and I became best friends with his daughter."[9]

Susan pioneered in another way in 1947, marrying Chief Petty Officer Francis Cuddy, an Irish American code breaker who helped in the fight for Korean independence from Japan. Many states at that time, including Maryland and Virginia, forbade marriages between races. So the Cuddys were wed in the U.S. Naval Chapel in 1947. Mrs. Cuddy later said: "The way to get your relatives to accept your mixed-race marriage is to have kids." She had a daughter, Christine, and a son, Philip. Susan Ahn Cuddy received a Woman of the Year Award in California in 2003 and the American Courage Award from the Asian American Justice Center in Washington, DC, in 2006.

Turn now to the story of one of the sugarcane workers in Hawaii, Soon Kwon Kim, who left Korea in 1906 for Hawaii and later made his way to Seattle and down the coast to Los Angeles. Soon Kwon Kim had been married in Korea to Nora Koh, who graduated from Ewha College in Seoul—which became Ewha Womans (cq) University after 1945. She wanted to be a college professor and so wished to further her studies in America. She arrived in Seattle with some missionaries in 1916 and wanted to continue college studies, but the U.S. immigration officer insisted that she had to join her husband. So Nora had to come south to L.A., where she joined Soon Kwon, and they began a family. Their daughter Willa Kim, who became a notable fashion designer, was born in 1917 at the home on Figueroa Street in Los Angeles. And in 1919 Young Oak Kim was born there. A remarkable war hero, Young Oak would earn the Distinguished Service Cross, two Silver Stars, two Bronze Stars, and three Purple Hearts, serving to the rank of colonel in World War II and the Korean War.

But before all that, Young Oak's parents, despite their education and ambitions, could only work as manual laborers. They did that work for a few years but managed to save enough money to buy a grocery store in downtown L.A. from another Korean immigrant who because of poor English could not communicate with salespeople or with customers. Soon Kwon Kim could speak English pretty well, and he and Nora made the store successful in an area of downtown where wealthy people lived, including early actors and directors of the pioneering film industry.

Young Oak Kim worked in the store while he attended grade school and then Belmont High. He went to Los Angeles City College for a year but dropped out, according to a biography, *Unsung Hero, The Colonel Young Oak Kim Story* by Woo Sung Han, a *Korea Times* journalist who researched and wrote the book in 2008. It was translated by Professor Edward Taehan Chang of UC Riverside and published in English in 2011. "Because of racial discrimination, Asian Americans were not given opportunities to pursue professional occupations, whether they had a college degree or not," the book reports.[10] So Young Oak Kim found work as a farmhand, meatcutter, and auto mechanic. When war broke out in Europe, Kim tried to enlist in the U.S. Army but was rejected because the army was not yet allowing Asians to serve. However, in January 1941, that policy changed and Kim was drafted into the army.

After he completed basic training, he was assigned to be an auto mechanic. "How come I can't become a combat soldier," Kim asked. "What, are you out of your mind," replied an officer. "You have the wrong eyes. Slant eyes won't make a real soldier."[11]

However, fate intervened on December 7, 1941, when Japan attacked Pearl Harbor, and army life and training became urgent and real. As Young Oak trained with his regiment, he gained notice. His company commander called him in one day and assigned him to attend Officer Candidate School at Fort Benning, Georgia. When Young Oak began his training there in November 1942, he was the only Asian—indeed the only minority—among the officer candidates.

Young Oak completed rigorous officer training in 1943 and was assigned to the 100th Battalion, an unusual outfit of Japanese American soldiers. Many of the soldiers' families had been sent to detention camps but the soldiers themselves served in the U.S. Army to fight in Europe. When Lieutenant Young Oak Kim showed up to join the 100th Battalion, an officer said, "I don't think you realize this is a Japanese unit. Historically, Koreans and Japanese don't get along. I'll have you transferred." But Young Oak refused, saying, "Sir, they're American and I'm American and we're going to fight for America. So I'll stay." Soldiers in the unit were standoffish in the beginning with the Korean American officer, but they soon developed trust and respect.

A while later, when the 100th was transferred to Camp Shelby in Mississippi for precombat training, Young Oak went to a detention camp in nearby Arkansas to visit families of friends of his from L.A. His biographer reports that Young Oak's mother had warned her son against associating with Japanese kids, but he had made friends in the neighborhood anyway. In telling these stories in the book, the biographer—and Young Oak himself—illustrate the contrast between divisions in the old world and possibilities in the new.

The 100th Battalion was soon put aboard a converted cruise ship and transported to Oran in North Africa to prepare for landing in Salerno, Italy. As the 100th moved up the peninsula toward Rome, it faced heavy resistance from German forces who were carrying on the war after Italy's forces had dropped out of combat. At a critical juncture, Young Oak and one of his men crawled through German lines and captured two German officers who then gave information that helped General Mark Clark achieve the liberation of Rome. Clark later promoted Young Oak to captain and awarded him the Silver Star.

The unit moved on from Rome to Monte Cassino, where in a fierce battle Young Oak suffered a bullet in his leg. He was treated at a field hospital and rejoined the unit, which shortly was transferred to France to fight in what became the Battle of the Bulge, one of the last great encounters of the war in Europe. In one of the battles, Young Oak received a severe wound in his hand, which became badly infected. He survived and could use his arm only because a quick-acting medical doctor poured a bottle of alcohol directly into the wound, stemming the poison. Then Young Oak's life was saved by penicillin, making him one of the first American soldiers to receive the newest miracle medicine.

After the war in Europe ended in May 1945,[12] Young Oak left the army and considered his opportunities in civilian life. He decided on an innovation of the postwar period and opened one of the first coin laundries in Los Angeles. The business was an immediate success, and Young Oak built it up in the late 1940s. But in 1950 war began in Korea, when forces of Soviet-backed North Korea invaded the U.S.-backed Republic of Korea in the South. Young Oak immediately left his business, rejoined the army, and demanded to be sent to Korea. As he put it in a local Korean newspaper, he saw an obligation "to pick up a gun and fight to help my father's country."

Some army generals wanted Young Oak to do intelligence work from Japan, but he worked through his friends from World War II service and got to Korea. There he was welcomed by President Syngman Rhee because Young Oak's father, Soon Kwon, had helped Rhee work for Korea's independence. Young Oak joined an infantry regiment that fought its way into North Korean territory but was then confronted by forces from Communist China. Battles continued between U.S. and Chinese forces in 1951. Young Oak was hit by shrapnel in both legs at a fight near the Yalu River and was airlifted to a hospital in Japan, where surgeons from Johns Hopkins worked critically to save his legs from amputation. They succeeded and when he recovered, Young Oak returned to Korea and was appointed commander of a battalion on the front lines and promoted to major. Truce talks commenced in Korea at that time, which ultimately created today's Korea of North and South states divided by a "demilitarized zone."

The fighting having ended, Young Oak went back to Ft. Benning to help train new officers. He then served in Germany, and in the early 1960s he returned to Korea to help the army of the Republic of Korea. He retired from the military in 1972 partly because he was suffering pain and disabilities from his many wounds. However, experimental medical treatments at UCLA helped restore his health so that he could lead a productive life.

And he did so for the next three decades, helping to create the Korean American Coalition, a Korean Youth Community Center, the Korean Health Education Information and Research Center, and other advances in the Korean community. He also worked to help his Japanese American comrades-in-arms develop the Go For Broke Monument commemorating their service in World War II in the 100th Battalion and the 442nd Regiment. Work on the monument began in 1991 and it stands today, listing the names of 16,126 Japanese American soldiers, near the Japanese American National Museum in L.A.'s Little Tokyo section.

Young Oak also extended his charitable work to social causes, serving as chairman of a women's shelter in Los Angeles in the 1980s, where he later spoke openly about a community problem. "Domestic violence," he said, "was a major social problem for every community. However in those days communities never wanted to publicly admit that domestic violence existed in their own backyards. Therefore it was extremely difficult to obtain support. Even if you persuaded people to donate, they wanted to do it anonymously."[13]

An extraordinary Korean American, Young Oak Kim died in 2005 at age eighty-six and was interred at the National Memorial Cemetery of the Pacific in Hawaii. Prominent Korean Americans worked in 2016 to have the White House honor him posthumously with the Presidential Medal of Freedom. But they did not succeed in receiving that honor, so they will try again in this and future years.

So what do these stories about two extraordinary individuals tell us? They tell us about immigration and America; Ahn Chang Ho worked tirelessly to free his native land but always counseled his fellow immigrants to adapt and become American. And Young Oak Kim, born in L.A., honored the country of his parents but devoted his life to fighting for America and then worked to help make it a better society, a better place. The lesson is that people immigrate to America for many reasons but often to live and act in new ways, not to keep the codes and customs of the "old country."

Times and events change everything. World War II—and the Korean War after it—made enormous changes to California and the West. The population of Los Angeles County alone more than doubled to over six million in the first decade and a half after World War II.[14] What had grown into a moderately interesting city, thanks to the movies and radio programs over the twenties and thirties, now blossomed into a major city, third largest and ultimately second largest in the United States.

The Los Angeles region became the center of the aerospace defense industry, of inventions and developments. Indeed, the very Internet that has revolutionized the world was invented by engineers and computer scientists working under contracts from the Defense Advanced Research Projects Agency, or DARPA. Briefly, with the United States and the Soviet Union facing a war of terrible destruction with intercontinental missiles, a new communications system that could survive a first strike and so retaliate was wanted. In Santa Monica, RAND Corp., working for the air force, came up with an idea for a distributed communications system, with no single command center but many outposts. Messages could find destinations by any route available.

Thus encouraged, the Pentagon awarded a research project in 1968 to computer scientists at UCLA, which was connected to the Stanford Research Institute and to UC Santa Barbara and the University of Utah. The project succeeded by 1969 in allowing institutions to transfer files between computers and to work simultaneously from different locations on shared projects.[15] It was called ARPANET, and within a decade or two it spawned the Internet, which has brought unprecedented communications ability to millions, including Chinese farmers now selling their produce to Shanghai or Seoul or Singapore or indeed to Los Angeles and all of California. These technological advances brought more people to California, and its sprawl of homes stretched farther and farther over mountains and deserts and shorelines. California, always expansive, became a giant.

The region and its growing population did something else: It turned America's focus more firmly to Asia. The United States had now fought in Asia to help China and defeat Japan. It had freed Korea, guided it toward a democratic republic, and worked to develop a democracy in Japan. It was involved in Asia, and attitudes changed at home as more Asian people came into California and the United States. For one thing, Japanese Americans, who shamefully had been sent to detention camps, came home to get back their land or to take menial work as gardeners and such. Then they sent their sons and daughters to college to become physicians and dentists and businesspeople, soon to bring radios, TV sets, and other appliances from their recovering ancestral land.

Korean soldiers who had fought alongside U.S. troops were able in the 1950s to migrate to America. Korean nurses were welcomed to work in California. Asian students came to U.S. colleges and universities starting in the 1960s. And some six thousand war brides of GIs came to America in the fifties and sixties and, by working to bring their relatives to the United States, fed a momentum of change in America's immigration laws.

The fact is that for most of the two centuries the United States had been keeping track of immigrants, it had barred Asians from immigrating to the country and from becoming citizens if they got here anyway. Indeed, until 1952 California had laws that forbade Koreans and other Asians to own land. The Supreme Court struck down those laws in 1952 as violating the U.S. Constitution. It was in 1952 also that the McCarran Walter Act revised U.S. immigration law. The law, named for Nevada Senator Pat McCarran, a Democrat, and Pennsylvania Rep. Francis Walter, a Republican, was frankly discriminatory.[16] Its aim was to fight Communist infiltration of the United States by giving the federal government authority to detain and prosecute suspected subversives.

But influenced no doubt by American society's belated acceptance of its Asian residents, the McCarran-Walter Act formally ended Asian exclusion. It allotted nominal quotas to Japan and other Asian nations. Importantly, the law eliminated race as a basis for naturalization and citizenship, making Japanese, Chinese, Koreans, and other Asians eligible to become citizens for the first time. McCarran-Walter in 1952 was the first step toward the great 1965 Immigration and Nationality Act that opened the way for all Asian populations to immigrate to America.

That 1965 law brought profound change to America by replacing an immigration system based on the National Origins Act of 1924, which was frankly discriminatory. The 1924 act was passed in reaction to decades of heavy flows of immigrants from Southern Europe—largely Italy and Greece—and from Russia and Eastern Europe—Czarist pogroms and political turmoil that sent many Jewish people fleeing to relatives who had settled in America (see *Fiddler on the Roof*). The 1924 law reduced immigration sharply by setting quotas that favored people from Northern Europe—Britain, Germany, Ireland, Scandinavia—and gave very small quotas to all others. Asian immigrants had already been limited by such laws as the Chinese Exclusion Act of 1882, which restricted the future immigration of Chinese laborers, but allowed Chinese immigrant residents already in the United States to remain. After 1924, immigration was sharply reduced in the 1920s and remained low in the Depression thirties and the War years of the forties.

But the postwar period brought new thinking about fairness to people who fought for the United States and for whom the United

States fought. And it brought demands for civil rights and voting rights laws to end discrimination against African Americans and others. Those political shifts opened the way for immigration reform and the 1965 Hart-Celler Act, which became the 1965 Immigration and Nationality Act. It was named for Emanuel Celler, a congressman from Brooklyn, New York, who as a thirty-two-year-old representative in 1923 opposed the 1924 law because it discriminated against Jewish people. Forty years later, Rep. Celler was head of the powerful Judiciary Committee in the House. He was joined in authoring the 1965 act by Senator Philip Hart of Michigan, a grandson of Irish immigrants who was so revered for his probity and skill that a Senate Office Building in Washington is named for him.

And the powerful backing that truly made reform happen came from President Lyndon Johnson, newly succeeded to the presidency following the assassination of John Kennedy. Johnson got civil rights and voting rights laws onto the books and now pushed for immigration reform. In a book entitled *The Law That Changed the Face of America*, Margaret Sands Orchowski, a journalist at *Congressional Quarterly*, recalls LBJ's 1964 State of the Union message, in which he called for reform so that "a nation that was built by immigrants of all lands can ask those who now seek admission: 'What can you do for our country?' We should not be asking them, 'In what country were you born?'"[17] A major point: LBJ was calling for an end to the National Origins system that had effectively given preference since 1924 to immigrants from countries of Northern Europe. In an era of civil rights reforms, that old way looked discriminatory.

However, a State of the Union speech does not make legislation. Politicking and compromise do. Opposition to a new immigration law arose in Congress out of fear that newcomers from Mexico and Latin America would take American jobs. So after debate, a limit of 120,000 annual entrants from Latin America was accepted in the new law, but that limit was ultimately exceeded by immigrants who came in through family reunification. Indeed, a basic argument in the run-up to the 1965 law was whether primacy should be given to attracting skilled people as immigrants or to family reunification. Family relationships won out in the law, which was signed at the Statue of Liberty in New York Harbor on October 3, 1965.

Yet that very issue, whether U.S. immigration law should emphasize skilled applicants or family members, remains at the heart of today's debates. The administration of President Trump avowedly favors reducing legal immigration and deporting all people living and working in the United States illegally. Yet what kind of legislation could gain passage in both houses of Congress is immensely uncertain. Arguments are loud as usual on all sides of the question, and divisions are prominent. Business groups and farm organizations favor more immigration not less, as the American workforce is aging in this period and labor shortages are showing up. Racial and ethnic prejudices are visible again, recalling more the spirit of 1924 than that of 1965.

Significantly, the U.S. population has changed in the last half century. In 1965 only 5 percent of the population was foreign born. In 2015, 13.5 percent of the current population, or 43 million people, are foreign born. Add the fact that newcomers from Latin America, Asia, and Africa have changed the complexion of cities and towns in all regions of the United States in the last half century. But then, with the passage of time, immigration statistics always surprise us.

Ironically, it was believed at the time that the 1965 law would not greatly increase immigration nor have any great impact on the makeup of the American population. That proved a historic understatement. Immigration totals grew to more than one million newcomers a year. And millions more came through expanded systems of visas for work or study and other qualifications.

The effect on the Asian American community was dramatic. In 1960, the Asian population of the United States numbered 980,000. It has risen to 19.5 million as of 2013, according to the Census Bureau. As a result of that law alone, the Korean community in the U.S. swelled from some 69,000 in 1970 to 1.07 million in 2000—and on from there to almost 2 million, as of 2016.

All who came were eager to enjoy at last the ability to immigrate to America. But the Koreans in particular were leaving behind a land recently devastated by the horrors of war and the desolation of its aftermath. South Korea swelled with families who had moved south from the North, which had been under the Communist rule of President Kim Il Sung and the Soviet Union since 1945. But Seoul was practically destroyed during the war, orphaned children roamed the streets, starvation threatened young and old.

Koreans tell many stories of that time. Mrs. Anne Kim grew up in North Korea as Young Rahn Cha, her maiden name.[18] She tells a story first of survival, then of struggle, and then of achievement. It begins as a harrowing tale but ultimately becomes a story of immigrants adapting and contributing to America.

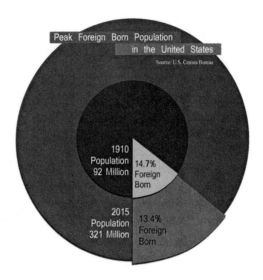

Chart shows high percentages of foreign-born population in 1910 and 2015–17 census estimates. High totals have led to political tension, then as now. Courtesy of Kris Delano.

"My grandfather was a wealthy man. He owned so much land near Yongbyon, where the nuclear base is now," Mrs. Kim begins, referring to North Korea's main nuclear science research center. "He made a deal with the Communists; he said I will donate some of my land but leave my family alone. My father was a doctor and he worked for the Communists too and also had his own patients." But such private deals with the state became untenable when North Korea's army invaded South Korea in June 1950. Young Rahn Cha and her family were still living in the North and were now faced with walking more than a hundred miles through battle zones to South Korea.

"We were late coming down—the war had begun," Mrs. Kim goes on.

I was eight years old in January 1951. We came together, my father and mother, my older sister and my younger brothers and sister. Also my father's brother and his newlywed wife were with us. There was no transportation—we were on foot. The young ones had to be carried on someone's back. I remember the bombing, the screaming and the crying. I saw a baby crying, but I did not see any parents. We had to grab my mother from the dust. If she had gone a little faster, she would have been blown up. She was a devout Christian and said

"God saved me," for she had so many kids to care for. We were really in the teeth of the war.

Indeed, the party was crossing the battle's front lines because North Korean forces after invading the South had pushed their way past Seoul, heading for the port of Busan, 250 miles south, in the first three months of the war. But U.S., South Korean, and United Nations forces under General Douglas MacArthur made a surprise landing at the port of Incheon, adjacent to Seoul, in late September and outflanked the North Korean forces, which had to fight their way back up the peninsula.

"My father became captive by the Communists," Mrs. Kim recalls. "They took him away from the family, and after that we never heard from him again. My mother had to take care of five kids. We were so poor." The War went on as U.S. and Korean forces moved into the North, fighting toward the border of Communist China at the Yalu River. Chinese forces then entered the war, and fighting continued until a truce ended it in July 1953.

In Seoul, "there was no business," Mrs. Kim recalls. "My mother had some jewelry her father had given her, and she sold that to live for a while. But that ran out. My young brothers and sister died of hunger. My older sister and I were left, and my mother had to start a business. She made a deal with factory owners to give her supplies, and she sold underwear at a giant market called Namdaemun, operating then in a northern part of Seoul.

"I had to grow up fast," Mrs. Kim recalls. "There was a mountain of trees that were being cut down for firewood, and I went to carry the wood on my back so that we could cook food. It hurt my back, but my mother said 'if you have the will, then you will do it.'" That of course is a motto of survival the world over, particularly among many who immigrate to the United States.

The mountain where she gathered firewood was an area that would later add to the campus of Seoul National University.[19] The institution was founded by the U.S. Army military government in 1946 by merging ten schools of higher learning around the Seoul area. The university suffered damage to many of its buildings during the Korean War, so the U.S. government and the University of Minnesota in a joint project with Seoul National undertook a restoration project from 1954 to 1960. And the young Ms. Cha—later Mrs. Kim—studied there, graduating with a degree in English. She also became engaged at that time to a young man named Dae Hoon Kim—who adopted the name David when he immigrated to the United States in 1964 to study civil engineering at the Illinois Institute of Technology (IIT) in Chicago. Korea began a rapid industrialization in the early 1960s after a military government under General Park Chung-hee took over in 1961. Park encouraged Koreans to study abroad and also to earn money overseas and help promote new products from Korean companies. Cha then followed her fiancé, immigrating to the United States in 1967 and going to Chicago.

There she received the rude awakenings that so many immigrants endure. Even though she had studied the English language at Seoul National University, Mrs. Kim found that she could not understand what people were saying to her—nor could they understand what she was saying to them.

"I applied to the University of Chicago to study for a master's degree in social work," she recalls. "But the examiner did not accept the transcript of my grades from Seoul National University. I said again, 'I am a graduate of Seoul National University,' but he said 'I don't know what kind of school that is, I never heard of that school, we cannot accept such a transcript.'

"So I enrolled at a community college to earn grades I could report to them. And I listened to the radio six months with a tape recorder to acquire some English. And I bought newspaper to read English. It took me two weeks!" she says with a laugh. But she succeeded. "We got married at that time and I went to the University of Chicago, one of the best, to study social work and psychology." David Kim attained his engineering degree from the IIT and worked for a large construction company in Chicago.[20] The Kims lived in the suburb of Skokie, Illinois, welcomed their first daughter, Sue Hee Kim, and joined a small Korean church. Yet Mrs. Kim tried also to attend another church where English was spoken lest she and her husband would "get too comfortable" in their own Korean community. "I would come home with a headache," she says.

Her determination to adapt to the new country is notable and would continue for years. David Kim was transferred by his firm, Kohler Construction, to St. Louis, Missouri. But while working for the large company, he opened a restaurant and hired a chef who could cook Japanese and Korean food plus some Chinese dishes. He saw the restaurant venture as a way to create an asset, a business he could sell, rather than a chance to enjoy Asian recipes. Mrs. Kim explained years later that "her David" understood that the temperamental chef would walk out sooner or later, so Mr. Kim taught himself to prepare some dishes and attract diners. Also he welcomed a freelance writer who reviewed new restaurants for the *St. Louis Post-Dispatch*, and the reviewer gave a writeup to this new kind of Asian restaurant in the 1970s. Mrs. Kim recalls that "people were lining up to come and try kimchi and Korean barbecue, which is spicy."

The restaurant succeeded and, following his original plan, Mr. Kim sold it and invested the money in founding his own small engineering and construction company. "We Koreans like to go into business for ourselves," Mrs. Kim says today. "When I came, I noticed opportunities are open in America. In Seoul, land is small, and metro areas are maxed out as far as people can have opportunities. But this is the best part of the world, with the American Dream."

That is not mere sentiment. In St. Louis, Mrs. Kim recalls, "there is a big shopping mall, Northwest Plaza. I was looking for a job, so I walked into every store and asked, 'do you have any job open?' They asked if I had experience, and then said 'I'm sorry, we do not have any position open.' Then I said, 'I will work free for one week and at the end let's talk job and money.'" She succeeded, of course, and was able to work at whatever task she was handed. "I work harder than anybody, sales, accounting, you name it—I do everything but rob banks," says Mrs. Kim.

David Kim's small construction company succeeded in the mid-1970s because the U.S. Department of Housing and Urban Development (HUD) introduced Section 8 housing to give low-income tenants a better choice of homes and apartments. Contractors could have HUD backing for jobs to improve and renovate residential premises. Kim succeeded, but within a few years he complained about the Missouri winters, where construction work is slow between December and March. "So he got a truck and drove to California," Mrs. Kim says. He sent for her when he had begun a new venture in repairing and renovating residences in enormous apartment complexes being built and developed in Irvine, California, at that time.

The Irvine Company has owned a huge block of land in Orange County since the nineteenth century, property that now holds half a dozen towns, major hospitals, and a University of California campus. The company developed Promontory Point in Newport Beach in the 1970s, a series of communities that consisted of thousands of leased apartments that needed repairs and refurbishing whenever tenants passed on or moved out. The company led by David and Anne Kim took on that work of painting and repairing residential properties and did well. "The agent in charge of property management would come to us and ask what happened to holes in the walls or broken masonry and damaged floors. And he would find that we had repaired them all," Mrs. Kim says. "We were very successful, and the more we did the more they gave us to do."

In good time, when their two daughters had moved on to college and successful lives, the Kims moved to Austin, Texas, and engaged in construction of new facilities for Wal-Mart Stores, Inc. "We went to Arkansas and talked to Walmart and then did construction services for the stores in Texas. They wanted to give us Louisiana too, but we had worked hard for many years and I said to David, 'let's retire and enjoy life,'" Mrs. Kim said, with a poignancy in her voice when mentioning her husband, who passed away in his seventies in 2014.

Mrs. Kim now lives part-time in Houston near her grandchildren and remains full of thoughts and opinions about immigrating to America—and about hard work, education, and overcoming obstacles. Here are some of her thoughts and strong opinions on Korea, on America, and combining attitudes and aspects of the two.

On Koreans and Americans: "I would love to motivate people who immigrate here, poor and colonized but with a passion for education. I always equate education with success. American people have never been through hard times with war and colonization and lack of opportunity," Mrs. Kim says. "And I sense a kind of laziness, a lack of appreciation for what they have. Koreans start small businesses, and when they make money they are proud that they have made it!"

On encountering prejudice: "If you look down on me, that is your problem, not mine. You may find prejudice, but if that makes you angry, turn that anger into hard work. I used to feel anger, but when I see my kids move up in the world, my anger dissipates," Mrs. Kim says. She is referring to her two daughters, one who heads recruiting for the Jesse H. Jones School of Business at Rice University and the other who runs her own consulting company while partnering in another business with her husband.

On customs from the "old country": "It is still a Korean tradition to be very polite, bowing and speaking reverently of older people. But that old way of speaking drives me nuts. I say my mind like the American way."

On coming to America: "I came here in 1967 and became a citizen in 1973. Not that many people from Korea here at that time; they would ask, 'are you lonely for Korea?' and I would say, 'no, I am more a here-and-now person.'" Over time, Mrs. Kim adds, she gained confidence. "I learned that I am a person who can adapt to anything. I just give my all in what is going on with my life at the time. I don't live in the past, but I try to adapt to the American Way. I did my best and I think my kids have that too."

Indeed, Korean immigrants of the sixties and seventies not only founded their own small businesses, but they helped to build up a few basic industries in America. Their sons and daughters are expanding today on foundations their forebears laid down.

CHAPTER 3

Newcomers Spur Industry, Earn Place in America

Recent decades have brought prominence to many things Korean. Large companies—Hyundai, LG, Samsung, and others—have invested and contributed to the U.S. economy, "from California to the New York Island," as Woody Guthrie's song has it. But it is immigrant entrepreneurs and their ventures that personify the energy and culture of Korean Los Angeles. To start with a major example, Korean immigrants have made Los Angeles the largest garment-making center in the United States.

The Korean Apparel Manufacturers Association (KAMA) was established in 1989 with six founding members.[1] Today KAMA represents some three thousand members in the broad fashion industry, which still includes sewing contractors, textile suppliers, and others. But the industry has changed. There are fewer traditional apparel manufacturing companies in Los Angeles, large firms making all the clothing and shipping to retail companies and stores. The pattern now is that fashions are designed in L.A. and manufactured abroad, whether in Bangladesh and Southeast Asia or in Mexico and Central America.

Yet a parallel phenomenon is that new companies are starting up all the time, designing and selling their fashions online, says Ilse Metchek, president of the California Fashion Association.[2] Los Angeles County, with more than 100,000 employees in apparel and related accessories industries, ranks first in the United States, reports the L.A. Economic Development Corp., a private nonprofit research organization.[3]

To understand this story, go back to 1963 at Incheon, the port of Seoul. The Republic of Korea's Navy plays rousing marches as working people board cargo ships bound for South America. Korea at that time was very poor. President Park Chung-hee had started the country's rapid economic development; the people were trained with rudiments of industrial skills. But there was little work at home and not enough food for an expanding population, so Park's government encouraged emigration. The first group of emigrants left for Brazil in 1963 with exhortations ringing in their ears. That in itself was new. Emigration was not a longstanding tradition in Korea.

Jung C. Choe, who later became publisher of *Pacific Textile News* in L.A., recalls the chants over loudspeakers: "Go and go and go, your country is too small for you. Go and find a place to live and prosper for the grander future of Korea. Learn something new, learn something better and useful. But do not forget your mother country. Plant Korean spirit there."[4]

The workers went to Sao Paulo, Brazil, where after a while they noticed that Brazilian neighbors admired what they wore—Korean-made clothes. So they sold what they had to the neighbors and began sewing "Made in Korea" garments at home. They sold the clothing door-to-door, and soon a Korean garment business blossomed in Sao Paulo.

Yet South America was not the Koreans' first choice. They wanted to immigrate to the United States for work and better education for their children. But immigration to the United States was difficult to impossible before the 1965 Immigration and Nationality Act was passed. Then thousands of Koreans began coming to the United States, setting up possibilities for relatives to join them. And from the mid-seventies through the eighties, many Brazilian Koreans migrated to Los Angeles. There they found the Los Angeles garment center of Santee Alley already expanding with textile facilities built by Iranian Jewish refugees who had fled Iran after the Ayatollah's Islamic revolution in 1978–1979. To the Koreans, the place was El Dorado. They bought garments from the Jewish manufacturers and sold them to swap meets in the Korean community. They pooled money in their communities of family and church connections and bought used knitting machines to set up factories—where they would sleep after putting in seventeen-hour days.

Soon local Korean immigrants swelled the industry, owners of liquor and grocery stores who found factory work easier and lucrative. "If you had a few friends who could put together a quarter million dollars, you could be running a $10 million knitting mill," explains one industry veteran. The Korean manufacturers worked on a cash basis— "where other makers look for a return on investment of 17 percent on orders," said David Kleinman, longtime garment industry owner and vendor, "the Koreans would take a job on 35 cents a yard cash margin."[5] They would turn out the garments, ship them to retail chains such as May Co. and J.C. Penney, and get cash immediately by financing the receivables—a transaction known as factoring—with a Korean-owned finance company such as Hana Financial. Then they would go back at it, turning out goods and taking cash in as fast as possible. In the seventies and eighties, said one textile executive, the Los Angeles industry was "like the wild, wild West."

"Wild East" might be more accurate. It was an industry of newcomers from a country that had been a colony of Japan until the end of World War II. The story of two pioneers, Sang Hoon and Eunice Kim, is told by their son Peter Kim,[6] who became a successful fashion producer in a later time. "My mother was born in 1942 and my father in '41, when Japan was at war," he says. Japan recruited some Koreans to fight in the war but mostly used Korea as a base for its navy to rule the seas down through its colony Formosa (now Taiwan) to the Philippines and the Malay peninsula (Singapore and Malaysia today). "They were born in what is now North Korea and were brought down in their childhoods to South Korea. It was not an easy passage," Peter says. "My father never knew his father, who went missing or killed in the war. My mother lost some siblings in the process of getting from North to South Korea."

Sang Hoon and Eunice Kim grew up during the Korean War and the devastation that followed in the 1950s. They came of age and wed in the 1960s and immigrated to Los Angeles in that decade. "They spoke no English, had no money but they worked hard at maintenance jobs, busing, parking cars, whatever they could do. And they saved as much as they could. They started a wig business in the early seventies," shortly after he was born, Peter says. "By pooling money with other members of their church, they started selling wigs in a shop. Then they found their way into fashion in the 1970s, and that proved a great time."

"They started a company called Protrend Ltd. that made 'Missy' blouses when women were first going into the offices as human resource personnel, working in accounting and legal staff positions. 'Missy' polyester blouses could be worn under suits with skirts or pantsuits. It was an incredible business that went from zero to thriving nationwide. All the moderate-priced department stores—Sears, May Co., Macy's—carried them," Peter explains.

"They made money and all their investors in the Church partnerships made money, and they invested in real estate," he says, recalling the energy of his parents and other immigrant newcomers who had known little but war and privation. Now they discovered large parts of the dream that has always drawn immigrants to America: They had the freedom to earn money and to join a church, to own a business and to invest in and own apartment buildings and offices. Los Angeles provided models for many Korean immigrants in that time—and then hard lessons, too.

Good times don't last forever of course. "The 1990s rolled around with 'dress-down Fridays' and less need for women wearing suits. Some products became irrelevant in the marketplace," Peter Kim goes on. "One big piece of their business got hit hard because some of the Protrend people got excited about promised sales and overbought inventories. There was a lack of management, and the company was stuck with hundreds of polyester dresses that were impossible to move, ended up with no value," he says.

Not only that, but Southern California suffered a post–Cold War recession in the early nineties, and real estate holdings of his parents and their investment partners got hammered. "I got into the business in 1994, I was twenty-three years old and in my last semester at usc," Peter says. "But business was depressed. We had real estate—condos in L.A. and New York and even shopping malls in Hawaii. It would be worth $500 million if we had it today, but we couldn't hold on so we sold off to reduce debt. We had no option to declare bankruptcy, Chapter 7 or 11," he explains, because that would have damaged not only his parents' credit ratings but those of their partners in the kehs or church investment pools. Finally, though, as conditions improved in the latter half of the nineties, he managed to wind down the debt and get the company and his parents free of it.

Challenges continued for the industry of course. In the 2000s cheaper garments from China flooded into the market and conditions became tough for many Korean firms, most of them small to medium size with five to fifty employees. The industry took a particular hit in 2014, when federal authorities raided the garment district for money laundering.[7] To explain: First the U.S. Treasury in 2011 put a limit on the size of currency transactions that could be done without registration and reporting. Vast sums could no longer move easily from U.S. drug dealers back to the Mexican cartels that wanted dollars converted into pesos. So the cartels ordered the dealers to pay dollars into garment industry companies for shipments of shirts and dresses to Mexican importers. The shirts and dresses then could be sold in Mexico and pesos paid to the cartels. Such schemes ended in September 2014, when more than a thousand agents of the fbi and irs and Homeland Security raided seventy-five locations in the garment district, arrested two dozen store and company owners, and seized $170 million in cash. Such a sum was a mere fraction of the $30 billion in drug money that flows annually between the U.S. and Mexico. But the raid was enough to force some fashion district firms to clean up their acts.

Yet for young Koreans and Korean Americans, there were opportunities as an industry matured and grew in several ways. Korean American designers brought fashion directly to Korean-owned retailers. Joy Han, for example, developed the off-shoulder dress style for her own Voom fashion firm and many apparel merchants.[8] When Han started out in the business, after graduating from Otis College of Art and Design, she was not immediately successful. Korean manufacturers said her styles were too forward, the tops and dresses "stuck out too much." But she persisted and won a following in Hollywood. "The design needs to stick out," she said, "the more so when the economy is bad." With her husband, James Kim, Joy Han also has a VaVa line of young women's apparel and a knitwear fashions as well. Interestingly, the couple includes quotations from Christian scripture and quotations from Dr. Martin Luther King Jr. and other spiritual leaders in its advertisements. Such aligning of strong religious faith and tough business acumen is a hallmark of many Korean businesspeople in the fashion industry and other endeavors.

Indeed, the founders of the most successful of all Korean-owned fashion companies, Forever 21, are known for going to religious services daily at 5:30 a.m. Do Won "Don" Chang and wife Jin Sook Chang immigrated from Korea in 1981, when both were in their late twenties.[9] Their first child, Linda, was born the year after, and the parents had to work hard—Don at a gas station and also as a janitor, Jin Sook as a hair stylist, a trade she had learned in Seoul.

But at the gas station Don saw Korean immigrants driving Mercedes and BMWs and learned that they were in the garment business. So he looked into it, and Jin Sook went to the top of a large hill and asked in prayer if she should open a dress shop. They opened a 900-square-foot store, Fashion 21, on North Figueroa Street in Highland Park in 1984. Jin Sook stocked it with tops, skimpy shorts, and skinny pants made by Korean manufacturers for teenage girls. She proved to have an eye for fashion and a fierce skill at negotiation. "My mother is an incredible buyer," daughter Linda, who now works for the company, told a business magazine a few years ago.

In its first year Fashion 21 took in $700,000 in sales, and the company, which changed its name to Forever 21, has gone on in the last three decades to become the fastest-growing clothing retailer to young women. It now has more than seven hundred stores in the United

Koreatown sign Los Angeles, also includes memorial to Dr. Sammy Lee, first Asian American to win an Olympic gold medal (in diving). Photo by Patricia Flanigan.

States, Europe, and Asia and had sales in 2016 of about $6.9 billion. Remarkably, it is still owned by two people, Mr. and Mrs. Chang, who have never sold stock to the public or taken the kind of giant financings from banks and investment companies that required formal disclosures on balance sheets. Daughter Linda, thirty-five, heads marketing for Forever 21, and her sister Esther, thirty, is in charge of graphics and window displays. "It's important my daughters learn from the hard work my wife and I put into this company," says Don Chang today.

Forever 21's success speaks of the energy and pride of Korean immigrants and of their deep religious faith that has helped a poor, subject people endure over centuries—as well as the opportunities of Los Angeles and America. In typical Korean fashion, daughters Linda and Esther Chang graduated from top-class universities—Linda from Penn's Wharton School and Esther from Cornell—while their parents never went to college. "Forever 21 gives hope and inspiration to people who come here with almost nothing," says Don Chang. He adds, with gratitude coupled with the deep pride typical of immigrants: "And that humbles me: the fact that immigrants coming to America, much like I did, can come into a Forever 21 and know that all of this was started by a simple Korean immigrant with a dream."

And yes, his words reflect belief more than sentiment. Every Forever 21 shopping bag carries a reference to "John 3:16" from the gospel of John the Evangelist. Those who look up the New Testament find the verse, "For God so loved the world that he gave his only begotten son, that whosoever believeth in him shall not perish but have everlasting life."

Even so, it takes more than hard work and deep faith to change the tough world of retailing. In Los Angeles, it has taken thousands of Korean garment makers, hundreds of stores and designers, sewers and trimmers, cutters and mills, and contractors, and the great energy of Santee Alley and environs to lead the revolution of Fast Fashion.

Forever 21 has been a leader in Fast Fashion, turning over inventory in its stores every three weeks—so that its young customers don't see the same merchandise the next time they visit. Hot items were put in the front of the store in limited amounts, snapped up, and then replenished by Korean apparel manufacturers who worked on short notice and short contracts. New ideas from designers everywhere were copied instantly. But where designer fashions at upscale stores might sell for $200 and up, Forever 21's price would be $29.80, $32.50, and so on. Forever 21 endured lawsuits over copyright infringement and settled out of court. Teenage and young adult women loved the stores. The business grew, and the company reached out to older customers, stocking varieties of women's fashions and also menswear. When Forever 21 opened stores in upscale shopping centers, the name over the door was put in "snobbish" Roman numerals—Forever XXI.

Awards came to Forever 21 from the Los Angeles Economic Development Corp. and others. And the company made investments that changed the landscape as well. In 1994, Forever 21 and a hundred other Korean apparel makers built San Pedro Wholesale Mart, a two-story center east of San Pedro Street, where more than three hundred garment makers sell fashions to retailers from all over the country and beyond.[10] The stores are all Korean owned but bear names like Cozy Couture, Mademoiselle, and other French words beloved of the fashion trade. "Women's fashions change very fast," says Don Chang, "retail is like a marathon, not a 100-meter dash."

However, recent years have seen some hurdles. Business has been less robust, and Forever 21 miscalculated its strength. When major retailers moved out of giant stores in some shopping malls, Forever 21 rushed in to take up such premises. It also opened 90,000-square-foot stores in New York and Las Vegas—more than twice the size of most of its outlets. It has had trouble using such space productively, and the company has closed some stores and is negotiating with mall owners to reduce its lease obligations.

Still, industry experts point out that Forever 21 stores in Shanghai and other cities in Asia are doing very well, and "the company really has nothing to worry about in the global market," adds Cal Fashion's Ilse Metchek. Forever 21 is and will remain a remarkable story, reflecting the strength of the Korean community and that of Los Angeles and America. A company founded in a small shop thirty-one years ago is credited today with having 10 percent of the entire U.S. apparel market. Don and Jin Sook Chang are estimated by *Forbes* to have a net worth of $3 billion.[11] They have established a Chang21 Foundation with the money and have reached out as donors and missionaries of the TtoKamsa Mission Church in Los Angeles, which supports churches of sixteen ethnic minorities here and sends missions to Central and South America and Africa. The Changs continue to serve on such missions.

Meanwhile, as the Korean American generations have carried on from their parents, they have brought "mainstream" financing into the business—private equity and venture capital, mergers, and public stock offerings. After Peter Kim stabilized his family's company by the early 2000s, he started his own apparel concerns. First he made T-shirts and hoodies with an outfit he named Drunken Monkey, which he then sold. He started Hudson Jeans in 2002 and over a decade and a half has built it into a denim brand selling at high-fashion prices to women and men at Saks Fifth Avenue, Nordstrom, and Neiman Marcus.[12] In 2013 he sold Hudson Jeans for more than $90 million into a new publicly traded company named Differential Brands Group, for which he handles the expanding Hudson Jeans line. But that has not been the only calling for now forty-seven-year-old Peter Kim.

Korean immigrants' children, like those of other nationalities, have brought a different spirit to their lives, one that often begins with anger. "As a kid, I was pissed off with a huge chip on my shoulder," Peter Kim recalls. "I was born and raised in this country but as Korean Americans, people would look at us as if we didn't fit in. And we didn't feel accepted anywhere. I just lashed out with anger stemming from the generational and culture gap."

Getting away from home didn't help either. "I first went to Southern Methodist University, but Dallas only furthered my feeling of being discriminated against so I came back to USC." In truth, the Korean Americans were experiencing only a last stage of the anti-Asian prejudice that has characterized U.S. society, particularly in California and the West, since the nineteenth century. The Korean immigrants' generation knew such prejudice and reacted by simply working hard and keeping to themselves. But younger generations have been determined to find a place in this society. "Things changed," Peter says, "and I began to think that I can either be a part of the problem or part of the solution. I worked very hard to fix the company and start my own companies. But also I became involved with One Voice"—an organization that helps underprivileged youngsters in the black and Hispanic communities to get through school and go to college and for families to deal with poverty and family problems. One Voice gives out furniture and clothing, as well as assistance in paying rents and obtaining housing. "It's not a matter of writing a check but getting your hands dirty and helping people," Peter says. "Empathy is important and compassion, get into someone else's shoes."

The next chapter will tell of violent events that inspired Peter Kim and other Korean Americans to involve themselves in all aspects of American society. But first, stories of two immigrants will tell of newly independent South Korea in the forties and fifties. Both men served in the Republic of Korea's army and then came to America. They built entrepreneurial careers in business, then in government, and turned to social and charitable work in Southern California. Their stories, often lively, sometimes poignant, add energy and vision to our American community.

The first is Chun Bin Yim,[13] who was born in 1942 in Seoul, where his father served on the Seoul City Council in the earliest days of Korean independence from Japan. Yim's grandparents on both his father's and mother's side were pioneers of banking and industry in old Korea. But as hostilities between Soviet-allied Communists in North Korea and backers of the U.S.-allied Republic of Korea in South Korea intensified, Yim's father was forced to flee southward and young Chun and his mother and siblings also had to escape Seoul on foot to Anyang, a community some twenty miles to the south. The Korean War followed from June 1950 to July 1953 before the family could return to Seoul. Chun Yim resumed studies in middle and high school, but his father lost a bid for reelection in the late fifties and then dissipated the family's money, buying back his council seat. "That's the way things operated in Korea; he returned to a political position, but our family had no money," Chun wrote many years later in his 2015 biography, which he triumphantly titled *I Will Work for Nothing*.

Indeed, in the 1960s his father deserted the family, and high school student Chun tutored other students to earn money. He took pride in the work: "Here I was still in high school and tutoring middle-school students whose parents desperately sought to get them into a good high school so they could then get into a good university. If this sounds like the educational system was stressful for your children, it was," Chun wrote. "But the tutoring was immensely helpful, for me as it enabled me to help my family. As the eldest son, it was important for me to support my family."[14] So, echoes from history, Confucian family codes are bred in the bone, and middle-class Koreans were early in facing pressures about schooling that now affect American parents and school districts.

Chun Yim won entry to Seoul National University, and in his junior and senior years had compulsory training in the Reserve Officer Training Corps of the Korean Army. On graduation he served as a lieutenant in the infantry, including a stint commanding a unit at the Demilitarized Zone—the 38th Parallel—between North and South Korea. It was dangerous duty then—and remains so today. Squads of North and South Korean soldiers would confront each other, often inflicting casualties, as civil war continued despite a formal truce. Chun served with distinction and survived to return to civilian life and win two big opportunities that changed his life. He won a scholarship to study anthropology at the University of Michigan. And he was chosen, after a stiff competition, to join a crew of young Koreans who would train American volunteers for the U.S. Peace Corps, which had been founded in 1961 by President John Kennedy.

The year was 1969, and the Peace Corps assignment took Chun to Hilo, Hawaii, where he trained and met volunteers, among them future U.S. ambassador to Korea Kathleen Stephens. The whole idea of the Peace Corps impressed Chun, and later in life he and Steven Choi, a fellow trainer who became mayor of Irvine, California, helped found Friends of Korea, a global organization that spreads Korean culture Peace Corps, style to many countries.

Then, with his University of Michigan scholarship and a student visa to the United States, Chun flew to visit a cousin, Chang Yim, who lived in San Diego. Long story short, Chun Bin Yim was about to choose an American future rather than the Korean professorship he was aiming toward in academia. Cousin Chang told him of opportunities in San Diego and suggested Chun scrap the idea of Michigan to study at San

Diego State and find work among the vibrant businesses springing up in California. "I asked myself, am I going to throw away everything I've done and start all over?" Chun later recalled that moment when he was twenty-seven years old. "I answered, *yes!* I could do this only in America, the land of opportunity."

And so Chun, who was later to adopt the name Charlie, took up an entrepreneurial life of facing and overcoming problems. At San Diego State he took English, math, statistics, and accounting. But he had to work to pay tuition and rent for his room, his cousin having moved to Atlanta. It happened that after his first semester he heard of jobs going at salmon-packing plants in Alaska. So he and a Korean friend drove to Seattle and flew to Nome, Alaska, but found no jobs in salmon-packing plants. But Chun went to a shrimp-processing plant and told a dubious manager, "I will work for nothing. If I do well, you can pay me after that." His job was to separate fish caught along with the shrimp in nets hauled in by the boats. He did the work; the plant took him on.

Back in San Diego, he used the same I-will-work-for-nothing tactic to land a job at the Aztec Restaurant on the San Diego State campus. The manager took him to the men's and women's restrooms and said clean them. Chun says, "I cleaned and cleaned until the restrooms were spic-and-span." The manager was impressed that a one-time Korean military officer worked hard at cleaning bathrooms and hired him.

However, the job led to trouble because Chun, on a student visa, was not supposed to work. He was summoned to the U.S. Immigration Office and told, "You are violating the immigration laws. We must deport you." The manager where he worked and the San Diego State administration office wrote letters supporting Chun. Ultimately, a professor saw a way out. He told Chun to transfer to Cal State Los Angeles, "where there are a lot of foreign students, many of them work, you will not be tracked down." The scheme worked and Chun Bin Yim, who had adopted "Charlie" as his American name, got to stay in the United States.

It was at that time in 1970 that Yim met Gloria Lee, the daughter of Dr. Sun Lee, a surgeon, trained in Seoul and the University of Pittsburgh, who helped pioneer microsurgery techniques and was then at the renowned Scripps Institute in La Jolla. But Dr. Lee and his wife did not want their daughter to marry Chun. They had a PhD candidate in mind for a traditional arranged marriage to Gloria—old world clashed with new. They banished Gloria from their home. But she rented a room, continued studies to become a teacher, and married Charlie Yim in October 1970.

They helped each other. Charlie completed his studies and got an accounting job at the City Hall of San Diego, where he worked for six years with Mayor Pete Wilson (later California governor) and others.

Charlie opened a small restaurant serving burgers and tacos near a high school. It succeeded, and he sold it within a year for $35,000, a goodly sum in the 1970s. Then he and Gloria bought and made a success of Ebb Tide Inn, a motel, even as they held jobs teaching and accounting. Thus the couple began a remarkable entrepreneurial career buying, improving, and selling 16 shopping centers, 5 hotels, 14 residential properties, and 4 small apartment complexes over the next three to four decades. They also bought parcels of land in developing San Diego County. And in 1985 they bought and made a success of Sierra Padre Mill Co., which makes doors and windows in standard and custom styles.

By 1986 Charlie Yim was prominent enough to travel with a delegation of San Diego officials and businessmen to Japan, China, and his own Korea, where he introduced the party to top executives of Samsung Group, LG Electronics, and Hyundai Motors—all were then expanding their presence in the United States.

Charlie and Gloria, parents of two daughters, had reconciled with her parents long ago. In 1975, they invited the parents to dinner, and Dr. and Mrs. Lee gave them a wedding ceremony at La Jolla Methodist Church. As the decades passed, Gloria and Charlie remained active. While teaching school at Camp Pendleton, Gloria earned a doctorate in education in 1993, and Charlie earned a doctorate in business administration in 1996. He wrote a thesis analyzing Korean small businesses, recommending that family companies step up to become more professional—more "American" in a word.

He has lectured students from all over the world who come to universities in San Diego seeking, as he puts it, the American Dream. "The American Dream is a reality," he tells them. "People from all over the world come to America searching for a better life and opportunity, better education. You are one of those lucky people and I am one of you."

"The I-will-work-for-nothing attitude is the spirit of entrepreneurship," he goes on. "It is creative, innovative, dedicated, passionate, courageous, and enthusiastic." Yim has won awards, notably the Presidential Award from the South Korean government in 2009 and the Presidential Award from the U.S. government in 2014.

He has donated millions to the Global Children's Fund of the Lions Club International and many other charitable efforts. "I came to this country empty-handed," Yim has said repeatedly. "And when I leave this earth, I will be empty handed."

But he is not done yet. In June 2017 he received the Hero of Ellis Island award, given since 2001 to individual immigrants or descendants of immigrants who have made notable contributions to America. Charlie's friends, former Governor Pete Wilson; Steven Choi, mayor of Irvine; and Judge Larry Stirling, of California's Superior Court, nominated Chun Bin "Charlie" Yim, American immigrant.

Move on now to Sukhee Kang, who immigrated to the United States in 1977 after completing his required service in the Republic of Korea's Army and marrying his wife, Joann.[15] His story tells a lot about the growth and prominence of the Korean community in California.

Kang was born in Seoul in 1954, just after the truce that stopped the Korean War. His father, Dae-Son Kang, was a merchant who owned a fabric store. Moreover, he was one of a traditional merchant class from Kaesong in North Korea who escaped from that region during the war and came to Seoul. Sukhee therefore grew up in relatively confident circumstances, went to good schools and to Korea University, where he excelled in English and engaged in public speaking. He listened to speeches of President John F. Kennedy and made it his ambition to come to America.

Yet when he arrived, first to his brother in San Francisco and then to a sister who was living in Santa Ana—in Orange County south of Los Angeles—Kang was perplexed to find he could not really understand what people were saying nor express himself easily. And he needed a job because he and Joann had moved into his sister's two-bedroom apartment with his sister's family, including a husband and four children.

Kang answered want ads for more than a month, applying for jobs with no success. He finally gained an interview for a job at Zody's, a discount department store that carried bedding, jewelry, TVs, and furniture. It was a chain that soon would become a part of Circuit City, a new kind of store that specialized in the sale of consumer electronics. As Kang tells the story, he got a call directing him to meet a Mr. Gimondo, a Circuit City general manager. In the interview Kang nervously explained that he had been in the United States only two months but that he spoke English well, having studied it in Korea. No, he admitted he did not have any experience working as a sales clerk. Gimondo seemed confused, Kang says, so he decided to go for broke.

"Mr. Gimondo, give me three months to work for your company and you won't regret hiring me," Kang said.

To Kang's surprise Gimondo smiled and said, "When can you start?"

"Right now," answered Kang. Gimondo smiled again and directed Kang to go for a few tests and be ready to report for work the following Monday.

So Kang started selling radios and eight-track tapes, earning $2.50 an hour and doing it well enough to win a sales award after the Christmas season. Significantly, when the company was handing out the sales awards in January 1978, Kang was hailed from the stage "as a very special person," not only for his sales record but for having come from Korea only months before. American society in Orange County was welcoming new immigrants and new businesses as consumer electronics firms—including Korea's LG and Samsung—were bringing advances to the Circuit City sales floors. In a book he later wrote titled *The Power of Possibility: My American Journey*, Kang recalled thinking amid compliments for being who he was as well as for his sales record: "This is America, when a person like me can be number one."

He found confirmation for that sentiment when he and Joann moved to their own apartment, admittedly in a poor neighborhood. They were robbed of everything they had, including a new color television set his sister had given them. But a coworker offered first to lend Kang money and when he declined gave them a used sofa because they had no furniture.

Kang continued to work hard and regularly came first in sales contests for Circuit City. He was soon promoted to selling color televisions and refrigerators for $500 and $600 a piece and received raises in his paycheck. Sukhee and Joann then moved out of their rental apartment and purchased a three-bedroom condominium in the city of Orange, a historic community that was growing with new homes and people in 1978. So the Kangs owned their own home only one year after his going to work for Circuit City—another milestone marked on the American Dream, and more were to come.

Within two years, Kang was transferred to the Circuit City store in Fullerton and shortly after named manager of the store in 1981. "I was the first person of Asian descent in the history of the company to be named manager," Kang says, "and at that time I was only twenty-six years old and had been with the company two and a half years." His success testifies to Southern California's growth in people and communities in those years and also to the forward thinking of the company's owner-managers. Circuit City was a pioneering company, founded as Wards TV stores in 1949 by Samuel Wurtzel and run in the late 1970s by his son Alan Wurtzel.[16] It was noted for intelligent management of its employees. "Instead of firing honest and able people who are not performing well, it is important to try to move them once or even two or three times to other positions where they might blossom," Sam

Wurtzel wrote for a book on management. And his son Alan said in a *Forbes* magazine article: "My father did not care how much education someone had or about race, as long as that person could work hard and sell on the floor."[17]

Sukhee Kang went on to manage several locations for Circuit City in the 1980s, but he noticed a change after the Wurtzel family turned management over to others. (Indeed his feelings were correct: Circuit City began a long decline about that time and ultimately went bankrupt.) Kang left Circuit City to sell cars for Hyundai of Korea, which opened U.S. operations in the 1980s, then was asked back by Circuit City but left again in the early 1990s for a new mission. He was asked to serve on the board of the Korean American Scholarship Foundation, which worked to help young Korean American students whose families had come upon hard times for one reason or another. The young people needed scholarships and guidance, and Kang became involved in the work. "I was a Korean American but had devoted myself to my work and raising my family and did not think the Korean community needed my help," Kang says. "But now I realized that my success gave me a responsibility to help others succeed in America as I was doing."

Within a few years, Kang formed the Korean American Democratic Council and became involved in local politics. He was now living in Irvine, one of the larger cities in Orange County—with more than 230,000 people, some 40 percent of Asian background—and began to work with its City Council. A locally powerful politician noticed Kang's abilities and made him a commissioner, an advisory post. Kang found not only that he liked politics but that he could achieve objectives. In an early example, Korean restaurants in Irvine had difficulty getting permits for the large exhaust fans needed to carry off smoke and heat from the open-pit barbecues embedded in their dining tables—a necessity for Korean-style cooking. Local officials couldn't quite understand the need for such powerful equipment—was it perhaps hazardous? They would have to think about it.

But Kang, of course, could explain and show the City Council how the equipment worked and why it was actually a safety feature of Korean Barbecue restaurants. "Just by having a place at the table, I was able to help the whole community, Korean and non-Korean alike," he mused in an interview recalling the matter.

In 2004 Kang ran for a seat on the Irvine City Council and won after developing an ability to campaign door-to-door. He would go to homes in neighborhoods, Asian and non-Asian alike. He was a Democratic

Party candidate but ventured into a strongly Republican community, rang the doorbells, and asked what the residents wanted to see in the community. Often he was thanked just for taking the trouble to visit the constituents of the city. He earned their votes and won election to the council and reelection in 2006. Then in 2008, Kang ran for mayor of Irvine. He won the election and became, as he likes to put it, "the first Korean American mayor of a major U.S. City." He won reelection as mayor in 2010 and served until 2012. Steven Choi won election to be mayor of Irvine after him.

Kang's public service included the customary duties of schools, businesses, and community issues. Also, he helped to bring public improvement to Irvine, such as its Great Park Project. But something more was pushing him. As he worked hard for Irvine and Orange County, he also consciously saw himself as furthering the causes of the Korean American community. He spoke of it in an interview and referred to it in his book *The Power of Possibility*.

> I made the decision to enter politics only when I became convinced it would be the best way for me to help the Korean community integrate into American society and achieve true equality. The more I immersed myself in political activism on behalf of the community, the more my affections for fellow Koreans grew. Although my responsibilities as mayor were to the Irvine community as a whole, I remained concerned with how I could improve the well-being of the Korean community and America's perception of it. And what I could do to improve the relationship between Korea and the United States.

Such talk combines gratitude for America along with affection for the country of one's birth and is typical of many leaders in public life over the years. Indeed, as a prominent Korean American politician, Kang helped start the movement in 2003 to have the centennial of Korean immigrants arriving in America in 1903 recognized nationally with a Korean American Day. The effort, joined by Korean Americans across the land, was successful and resulted in a proclamation approved by the House and Senate of the U.S. Congress in 2005 and signed by President George W. Bush, with Sukhee Kang among a delegation of Korean Americans in attendance.

Yet a question remains: Why did Peter Kim, Charlie Yim, and Sukhee Kang, three successful businessmen, turn to social work and politics at a point in the early 1990s and beyond into the present?[18] One answer is the Los Angeles Riots of 1992. The riots delivered a terrible challenge to Korean Americans in California and the U.S.—and indeed across the world.

"My initial reaction was pick-up-a-gun-angry, but that's when I thought I can be part of the problem or part of the solution," says Peter Kim.

"In 1992, the L.A. riots seared my heart," says Sukhee Kang. "I felt a great injustice had occurred, and I had to get involved because I could either watch and do nothing or learn and become someone. 1992 changed my life."

The next chapter will tell of the L.A. Riots and how the Korean community responded. It was a turning point.

CHAPTER 4

Rude Awakening
to American Dream

At the beginning of the 1990s, the Korean community in Los Angeles County may have numbered about 200,000 of the 800,000 Koreans counted in the 1990 national census. Perhaps another 80,000 Koreans had settled then in New York City, mainly in the borough of Queens. Mostly they were a mix of longtime residents, Korean War veterans who had earned visas, Korean War brides who had brought over their relatives, and new families who had been able to come after passage of the 1965 Immigration and Nationality Law.[1]

They worked hard to save money and buy their own businesses, hoping to earn enough to send their children to good schools. In some cases, they opened swap meets where they could sell goods for cash, although such markets originally were on barter, trading clothing and household goods. Grocery stores also were a popular choice for Korean newcomers. Families could work together; children could help out after school. In the New York area, Korean-owned fruit and vegetable stands were attractive and popular, gracing storefronts in many parts of the city. In Los Angeles, however, regulations allowed grocery stores to get licenses to sell liquor, beer, and wine, and that was a profitable attraction for Korean buyers. As a result, more than two thousand liquor and grocery markets in the Los Angeles area came to be Korean owned. In many cases, the Korean owners took over stores in poor areas of South Central L.A. that had been left behind by Jewish owners after the Watts Riots of 1965.[2]

True enough the locations added risks to the business, and cultural differences often compounded those risks. In New York an incident in 1990 involving a Korean owner of a grocery store named Family Red Apple got into a dispute with an immigrant woman from Haiti in the Flatbush section of Brooklyn that led to an eight-month boycott of that store and other Korean groceries in the city.[3] The Red Apple case was a sign of tensions between Korean grocers and African American residents who were their customers. That same year of 1990, Korean newspapers reported armed robberies at thirteen Korean-operated stores in the Los Angeles area. The Korean American Grocers Association counted nineteen killings of Korean store owners in the previous decade. Famed Korean American journalist K.W. (Kyung Won) Lee, editor of the *Koreatown Weekly* and then the *Korea Times Weekly* from 1979 into the nineties, chronicled the "hardy Korean mom and pop storekeepers" who "lived dangerously every waking hour in the seething inner cities of America."[4]

By the same token, the African American customers often felt suspicion and dislike from reticent shop owners. "They never smile or say thank you, they won't let you use the restroom and they overcharge," said Gina Rae, an African American Los Angeleno involved in social causes for her community at that time.[5]

And yet common humanity often overcame such stereotypes.[6] Choon-an Song, a Korean immigrant who ran a grocery store in South Central L.A. with her family, spoke warmly of her African American customers. "We became close and friendly with some of our black customers and their children, sometimes they even became like family," she said. Such are the paradoxes of diverse urban societies that division can melt before human kindness even as it can flare to anger before tribal suspicion and difference.

So it's important, given those paradoxes, to consider a scholar's explanation of the forces driving many Korean immigrants in the early 1990s—because they were soon to face a cataclysm that was to change the Korean community and the city of Los Angeles. Professor Edward Chang of UC Riverside spoke of his community in a book written two decades ago. "Typically, Korean immigrants are motivated by two concepts: *han* and *jung*," said Professor Chang. "*Han* relates to experiences of oppression like that suffered under Korea's long occupation by the Japanese and to rage and frustration. Koreans attempt to release han by working hard to make the American dream come true."[7] But jung, he went on, "encompasses feelings of love, compassion, sympathy, and sentiment. It drives Koreans to work together and to bring even distant relatives from Korea to live with them in the United States." Koreans of course feel special about their han and jung, but every immigrant group can identify with similar feelings, from the urge to belong in a new society to the tribal comfort of being with *your own kind.*

Let's move now to sparks that lit a long, consuming fire. In March 1991, a man named Rodney King held up a Korean liquor store in Monterey Park, a city eight miles east of downtown L.A. Los Angeles police pursued King, caught and beat him in a struggle that was recorded by a video camera that went "viral," as the current word would put it, not simply throughout the city but across the nation and the world.

Then thirteen days later, on Saturday morning March 16, a fifteen-year-old African American girl named Latasha Harlins went into Empire Liquor Market Deli to buy a container of orange juice.[8] The store was on a stretch of Figueroa Ave., south of Manchester Boulevard in South Central Los Angeles. It was owned by Korean immigrants Hung Ki Du and his wife, Soon Ja Du, who was behind the counter that morning, serving two children who were buying hair gel for their mother. In a very detailed account of that morning in *Official Negligence*, a book about the Los Angeles Riots written in 1997 by journalist Lou Cannon, Latasha took the carton of orange juice from the refrigerator, put it in her backpack, and headed to the counter with $2 in her hand to pay for the juice. But Soon Ja was a nervous woman who distrusted black people and the neighborhood. The Empire Deli had been robbed the previous Saturday when Hung Ki—who called himself Billy—was in charge and robbed also in December 1990 by black gang members. "Are you trying to steal my orange juice?" Soon Ja asked Latasha.

"No, I'm not," Harlins replied. "I'm trying to pay for it." And she turned to show the Korean woman her backpack. But Soon Ja reached across the counter and grabbed Latasha's sweater. "Bitch let go," Latasha shouted. "I'm trying to pay for it." But Soon Ja screamed, "Bitch, you are trying to steal my orange juice," and shouted for her husband, who was sleeping in a van parked outside the back of the store.

Events at that point—that were recorded on an in-store security camera—went from bad to worse. Latasha's backpack swung from her shoulder and fell to the counter. Soon Ja pulled it away. Then Latasha punched Soon Ja three times in the face, knocking her to the floor. But she came back with a chair, which she hurled at Latasha, who moved closer. Soon Ja reached under the counter and pulled a revolver from a holster. Latasha reached down to pick up the orange juice, which had fallen to the floor. She placed it on the counter. Soon Ja knocked it aside with a swipe of the gun.

When Latasha saw the gun, she turned and began to walk away. "Harlins knew what guns could do," wrote author Cannon in *Official Negligence*. Latasha's mother, Crystal Harlins, had been shot to death at a nightclub when Latasha was nine. But bracing herself on the counter and using two hands on the pistol, Soon Ja fired a single shot at the retreating girl, who was less than four feet away. The bullet struck Latasha in the back of the head and exited through her forehead, killing her instantly. Soon Ja's husband, Billy, awakened by the shot, rushed into the store to find Latasha's body lying on the floor and his wife saying there had been a robbery. Billy phoned 911 and told the police dispatcher, "We got a holdup." And the account of what went on from there goes for a full chapter in *Official Negligence*, a seven-hundred-page book with the resounding subtitle *How Rodney King and the Riots Changed Los Angeles and the* LAPD.

Police officers and detectives arrived and took possession of the videotape and gun and other evidence from the store. Soon Ja Du told them she feared the black girl had a weapon in her knapsack. But police searched the pack and found only some clothing and a few toiletries. As a young girl had been killed by Soon Ja's gunshot to the back of her head, the storekeeper was charged with murder and the case went to a grand jury. The case initially received little publicity beyond Los Angeles, where local news was still dominated by the Rodney King beating. Still, even though gunfire and violent death were commonplace in the South Central area, there was grieving in the African American community because the death of young Latasha seemed so senseless. The girl, who lived with her aunt and grandmother, had no criminal record and indeed was a pretty good student at Westchester High School. She hoped one day to become a lawyer and had written a school paper about the concerns of families living in poor, violent areas like South Central. The community consoled itself with the belief that justice would be done, and the storekeeper who had killed the girl would be tried and convicted at least of manslaughter and sentenced to prison.

Indeed Soon Ja Du was found guilty of manslaughter in her trial, which ended on October 12, 1991, and faced a sentence of up to ten years in prison.[9] At the sentencing hearing the following month, the prosecutor Roxanne Carvajal and Latasha's grandmother Ruth Harlins spoke for a strong prison sentence. But under California law, a judge has broad discretion over sentencing guidelines. In this case, Judge Joyce Ann Karlin, presiding over her first jury trial, prepared a speech that regretted the killing of Latasha Harlins but argued that sending Soon Ja Du to prison would not serve to foster healing between the communities. And at that she suspended prison time and gave Soon Ja Du five years probation with four hundred hours of community service. The courtroom erupted with cries of "Thank You God" in Korean and shouts of "murderer" from the Harlins family and friends. Sheriffs' deputies moved in to quell fighting between Koreans and African Americans. Outside the courtroom, Ruth Harlins said the probation "was an injustice." Resentment has run deep in the black community ever since—vigils were held in Los Angeles in 2016 to commemorate the twenty-fifth anniversary of Latasha's death and to preach against injustice.

Resentment strongly fed the flames five months later on April 29, 1992, when news came that the police officers who had beaten Rodney King were acquitted of any crime, in a trial held in Simi Valley. Riots broke out at the intersection of Florence and Normandie Avenues, when African American rioters attacked cars and dragged Reginald Denny, Felix Lopez, and Sai-Choi Choi, a Chinese immigrant, into the street, beating them severely. But the men were saved by other African Americans who stepped in at risk of their own lives to get the victims to safety at hospitals or fire stations. Stunned by the ferocity of the outbreak, Los Angeles police in patrol cars did not step in but retreated, hoping to organize reinforcements. In the confusion, the situation got completely out of control. "Mobs ransacked and burned at will," reported *Official Negligence*. "They were especially destructive in attacking Korean-owned stores which were demolished with a ferocity reminiscent of attacks on Jewish owned shops in Nazi Germany."[10] The riots went on all night in South Central while the LAPD continued to fumble in confusion. Ironically, the Empire Market Deli, which had been boarded up since the Latasha Harlins killing, was not destroyed but only because residents of a neighboring black-owned motel were threatened by flames.

As the riots spread in central Los Angeles, Korean store owners gathered whatever they could carry, and fled. Meanwhile, television news—reporting from helicopters—continued to show the fires and looting. And that aroused young Korean Americans to want to help their compatriots. In a video entitled, *Sa I Gu*—which means 4-2-9 (April 29) in Korean—Jung Hui Lee recalled her son Edward Song Lee saying, "Mom, we can't sit still, we must act," as he started to rush off to South Central that evening.[11] She feared for her son, Ms. Lee explained, but told him a tale from history of Korean women carrying rocks in their aprons to defend the town of Hangju against the Japanese. That only inspired the son to repeat, "Mom, we can't sit still" as he left with friends to go help store owners. But there were two groups of armed young Korean Americans on the same kind of mission that night. When one group fired in confusion at the other, Edward Song Lee, nineteen years old, took a bullet in the head that came through his windshield and was killed. He became one of fifty-three persons killed among many more injured in what became five days of rioting that destroyed twenty-three hundred Korean-owned stores, swap meets, and other property.

Things were different in Koreatown,[12] where Korean storeowners were less isolated and well armed. Some had received military training in Korea, and a few members of the older generation were veterans of the Korean War. Richard Rhee, who became a leader of Korean resistance in the riots, was one example. Rhee had come to Los Angeles in 1957. He spoke no English but found work as a dishwasher in a Chinese restaurant by day and a janitor by night. He learned English well enough to study business at UCLA and he saved enough money to buy a garment factory, which he sold at a profit, and bought a neglected Mayfair grocery store near Fifth Street and Western Avenue. He transformed that store into the California Market, a large-scale grocery that featured Asian delicacies.

By the time of the riots, Rhee was a wealthy man with many properties but devoted to his California Market. He was in his office when the riots began. He saw the beating of Reginald Denny on CNN and told his security people to gather reinforcements. By nightfall he had posted guards with loaded guns on the roof and assembled twenty armed men in the parking lot, where he ate and slept behind a barricade of trucks and luxury cars. A police car pulled up at the market on the first night, Rhee reported, but left after seeing that the Koreans seemed capable of defending themselves. Similarly at a nearby mini-mall at Santa Monica Boulevard and Vermont Ave., Jay Rhee (no relation to Richard) and his employees held off rioters by firing rounds into the air. Police officers drove by, Jay later reported, but did not come to help. "We have lost our faith in the police," he told the *Los Angeles Times*. "Where were you when we needed you."[13]

"Where were the police?" became a refrain among Los Angeles Koreans. "Koreans paid their taxes and were entitled to police protection," said Soon Cho, an editor at the *Korea Times*, "but they got betrayal by the police instead."

"The police did not help us. My mother worked at a swap meet in South Central that was destroyed, my father lost his job at an auto dealer in Koreatown," said Erick Yi, who became an investment manager at Merrill Lynch and today owns a business producing spicy sauces for Korean restaurants. Shock and fear spread among Korean communities nationwide.

So what did happen to the police in the Los Angeles Riots of 1992? The immediate answer is a variety of miscalculations and misunderstandings. As police units tried to gauge and combat levels of rioting around central L.A., one squad retreated to assemble reinforcements. Chief Daryl Gates was out of touch for several hours—at one point in a helicopter surveying the violence but not communicating with headquarters. Both Mayor Tom Bradley and Gates mistakenly thought the riots would start to peter out during the first night because they recalled something like that happened during the Watts Riots of 1965. They did not reckon with the buildup of resentment in the African American community since the Rodney King beating and the Latasha Harlins probation verdict. A postriot federal commission, headed by former FBI and CIA director William Webster, found that no preparation had been made for protests after the trial of the police in the King beating ended. Also, the LAPD was slow to ask for help from the Los Angeles County Sheriff's Department—and the Sheriff was slow to give help. It took until the third day to respond to Governor Pete Wilson's offer of activating the National Guard. Meanwhile, Mayor Bradley had asked for federal troops, who also came to Los Angeles. One way or the other, with National Guard and U.S. Army and Marine troops on patrol, the riots ended by Sunday morning, May 3. Property damage was later calculated at $800 million—with $400 million of that destruction to Korean-owned property.

It was a profound blow to the Korean community. At the most basic level, people who had worked and saved to buy a grocery store, a dry cleaners, or other business were faced with a loss of life savings. A good many Koreans of the immigrant generation were ready to throw in the towel and sadly say that America was not for them. But something else emerged also. The younger generations of Korean Americans, who had come as children or were born here, awakened to membership and spirit in the Korean community. Indeed, "the Korean American was born or reborn on April 29, 1992," wrote Professor Chang of the L.A. Riots, which continues to be called Sa-I-Gu (4-2-9) in the community. The Riots served, wrote Chang, "as a catalyst to critically examine what it meant to be Korean American in relation to politics, race, economics and ideology."[14]

It was not an academic exercise but a call to action. At the very start, while the majority of shopkeepers were bewildered, as they were not fluent in English or educated in matters of law and insurance policies, help arose from Korean American lawyers who made pro bono commit-

Violence Flares at Florence and W. Normandie Avenues. Police retreated from the intersection for hours. Photo taken by Kirk McKoy. *Los Angeles Times*, April 22, 2012. Courtesy of the *Los Angeles Times*.

ments. John Lim was president of the Korean American Bar Association of California when the riots began.[15] Lim had come to America with his parents at age ten. He went to school in Koreatown but then was bused to middle school in North Hollywood, where he found prejudice for the first time in his life. It made him ambitious to work in finance and the law for minority issues and businesses. He studied accounting at Cal State Northridge and then earned a law degree at the University of California, Hastings College of the Law. He founded the Lim Ruger Law Firm in 1986, when he was twenty-nine.

In an interview for this book, Lim recalled,

At the time of the riots, there were probably 100 Korean American lawyers who were bilingual while most of the victims had limited English and all their eggs in one basket. There was a huge need for legal assistance dealing with insurance policies, small business loans and a host of other issues. So we had a meeting of the Bar Association on the first night of the riots and unanimously decided to mobilize a pro bono legal clinic of eighty or so lawyers who would donate two to five hours a week of legal services for victims of looting and destruction.

The lawyers' work helped in the immediate aftermath of the riots and continued to help as Korean store owners encountered political and judicial opposition in efforts to rebuild their businesses.

Political opposition to rebuilding liquor stores grew in the wake of the riots, and the California legislature passed ordinances restricting liquor licenses. Such restrictions were then upheld in lower courts and the California Supreme Court, causing Korean store owner Sung Ho Joo, whose business had burned down, to exclaim, "this is like a second riot—this time in the hands of the highest judges in the state."[16] Lawyer John Lim even today recalls acidly that "it was easy in the atmosphere of that time to blame gang and family problems on alcohol consumption and on the Korean stores that sold the alcohol. But big supermarkets did not cut back their sales of alcohol."

Nonetheless, the aftermath of the 1992 Riots brought great changes to the Korean community and to the Los Angeles Police Department. The LAPD began years of reform under terms of the Independent Commission on the Los Angeles Police Department, which was created by Mayor Bradley in 1991 after the beating of Rodney King. Bradley appointed lawyer Warren Christopher to lead the commission, which delivered its recommendations a year later, after the riots. The Christopher Commission Report, as it was called, recommended a shift to community policing, an end to racial discrimination, and other reforms. It also recommended that Chief Daryl Gates be replaced. He was more or less forced to retire in June 1992.

The LAPD truly did adopt community policing in the decades that followed. And in April 2017, on the twenty-fifth anniversary of the riots, Chief Charlie Beck—who served as a sergeant in 1992 and became head of the department in 2009—wrote in the *Los Angeles Times*: "We now believe that there is no true public safety without public trust, that serving the Constitution by protecting the rights of individuals is the ultimate goal of policing and that relationships and partnerships are essential to policing in our city. The LAPD and I were forever changed by the 1992 riots."[17]

Fortunately and dramatically, the shock and bewilderment of the riots brought even greater and lasting change among Koreans and Korean Americans. Within days of the riots, there was an unprecedented

Peace March in Los Angeles by more than thirty thousand Korean Americans. The community began to look about and reach out. "We had to bust out of our cocoon," said Tong Suhr, an attorney in Los Angeles. "This country is made up of people from all over the world. We had to learn to live in harmony with all the other people, not just Koreans." Immediately Korean American organizations formed in California and across the country, with such names as The National Association of Korean Americans and the Korean American Coalition. It was a rude awakening, said Tammy Chung Ryu, who was a supervisor in the Los Angeles County attorney general's office at the time of the riots and is today a Superior Court judge. "We had thought we were doing well economically, with good jobs and education—but we had no voice. At the levels of political power, we were not listened to."[18]

It was in that postriot time that journalist K.W. Lee, himself an immigrant who came to the United States in 1950, dispatched his younger Korean Americans with marching orders: "Individually we are powerless and dysfunctional," he wrote. "But YOU must be the generation to create a new value system—one of community consciousness—to break away from the past."[19]

And the generations responded.[20] "Young people saw the police and government and all the positions of power, and the Koreans had none of that in the nineties," says John Suh, president of LegalZoom, Inc., a high-tech company that provides lawyer-free help with legal documents such as wills and trusts. "It was a wakeup call," he says. "Koreans are not insular culturally, but that is what other people saw. So we had to engage the community, to reach out and establish bridges."

"Now we are in the police and the government, and we have reached out to other people," Suh adds. "The environment is much better today, much better than it once was." Similarly, John Lim and his law firm went on to serve global corporations as well as major Korean community projects in Los Angeles and also to help create a national council of Korean Americans, with a staff to lobby the federal government in Washington (see chapter 6).

The environment is better thanks to many extraordinary Korean Americans who started projects that brought the Korean community into social and charitable work for all the peoples of Los Angeles and U.S. society. A tradition of reaching out that began in the L.A. Riots has carried on through the decades and is primed to continue for the future.

A notable example is Spencer Kim, chief executive of CBOL Corp. in Chatsworth, which manufactures high-tech equipment for the aerospace and defense industries in the United States as well as countries of Asia, Europe, and Latin America.[21] At CBOL headquarters in the San Fernando Valley, a workforce speaking fifty-one languages caters to customers in countries across the world. His employees are "immigrants and from immigrant families," Kim explains, working with modern computer and communications technology to serve the U.S. State and Defense Departments. He takes pride in the firm's global outlook; "it is like all of Los Angeles," he says.

A global outlook informed his reaction when the riots hit in 1992. Kim started Project Bridge to teach young people about Korea and the wide world. In partnership with the Korea Society in New York, Project Bridge spreads knowledge of Korean culture among young Americans. The program chooses sixteen high school students every year—eight from the Los Angeles area and eight from New York—teaches them in seminars and leadership classes, and sends them on ten-day tours of South Korea to learn about language and culture as well as art and customs.

The purpose, says Mr. Kim, "is to inspire cultural awareness and teach the importance of understanding between cultures so that Sa-I-Gu cannot ever happen again." The students come from diverse backgrounds and they visit Seoul and other cities, learning about the people and their systems of education and politics, entertainment, cuisine and daily lives. They visit Korea in May and return in June to a reception in Chatsworth, where they tell their parents and friends about what they've learned. Asked to compare their new knowledge of Korea and Asia to what they've learned in their high school classes so far, some students said they were taught in the latter about "France and Spain" but not much about China, Japan, and other countries. However, that is changing as more schools in the Los Angeles area are teaching about Asian languages and cultures.

Spencer Kim himself was born in Seoul in 1946 and came to the United States in 1963 for high school in Seattle. He studied engineering at Seattle Pacific University and the University of Washington as well as business at Washington State University. He has founded numerous companies over the last forty years as well as serving on U.S.-government-backed committees and missions concerned with Asia Pacific Economic Cooperation. He started the Pacific Century Institute in Los Angeles in the 1990s. The institute, with several U.S. ambassadors to South Korea and other government officials on its board, sponsors efforts to help reunite South and North Korea. Kim has visited North Korea several times in the last decade. Contrary to conventional opinions, Spencer

Kim thinks that South Korea and the United States should open more contacts with the North, even help its economy, as West Germany did for East Germany in the four decades of the Cold War. He believes both North and South Korea "dream of a united Korea taking its proper place in the Asian constellation." So even amid current threats about nuclear weapons from the Pyongyang government, Kim believes "it is time to talk and keep talking until the deal is done." (More on North Korea in chapter 7.)

The president and chief executive of Superior Grocers, Mimi Song, is an early postriot organizer of Korean philanthropy for other communities.[22] Born Mi Ryong Song, Mimi immigrated to Los Angeles with her family in 1977 when she was twenty. She started work in a grocery store in South Central L.A., but by 1981 she and her sister and their uncle James Oh had started Superior Grocers in an old store in Covina. Today Superior has forty-five stores in the greater Los Angeles area and more than $1 billion in sales. Superior's stores, the majority of them in Latino neighborhoods back then, were not looted or bombed in the 1992 Riots. But in 1995 Mimi started a charity, the Community Re-Engineering Co., through the Superior Foundation. The charity concentrates on helping underprivileged youngsters through charter schools, the United Negro College Fund, City of Hope, and other charities. Admittedly the idea for the charity came in the aftermath of the riots. Still, Song was early in philanthropy beyond her Korean community. "As an immigrant, I feel a special responsibility to other immigrants," Song has said.

At the time of the 1992 Riots, Hyepin Im was studying for an MBA at USC's Marshall School of Business and working part time to raise capital for the Rev. Mark Whitlock of the First African American Methodist Episcopal Church.[23] She wasn't working directly for the church, but for its FAME Renaissance Capital nonprofit corporation, through which it raises money to help parishioners qualify for mortgages, buy residences, and learn about the intricacies of housing finance whether for renting or buying. The existence of FAME Renaissance as an affiliate of First AME, the oldest African American Church in Los Angeles, was an eye-opener for Im.

She is the daughter of immigrants from Korea who became ministers and founded a church, one of the more than fifteen hundred Korean congregations in the L.A. area. "My Mom was a faithful follower, but my Dad was a nonbeliever," Im says in an interview. "As a condition of their marriage when they came to the U.S., he agreed to learn about the faith and found he had a calling. He started his own church where they preached the Word but also many times served as unpaid social workers for their church members, even though they had few means and resources."

Hyepin Im, born in 1966, studied business management at UC Berkeley, graduated in 1988, and returned to work with her parents and members of other poor Korean congregations to find ways to pay for affordable housing and help with family problems. Rev. Whitlock's FAME Renaissance was an answer, she saw; it could raise contributions from private corporations and grants from government institutions because the money was not going to any specific religion or church but to a nonprofit corporation working to help communities and citizens. "Because the church's affiliate could connect with the greater community," says Im, "it could bring in additional millions of dollars."

In the 1990s, Im worked to raise funds for the California Science Center, and in 2001 she founded Korean Churches for Community Development (KCCD), a nonprofit corporation that combines resources from Korean Churches and the greater community of corporations and government institutions. Also from 2001 to 2004 she studied with the Wesley Theological Seminary in Washington, DC, to earn a master's of divinity degree. Since then she has taken KCCD to considerable heights. She has linked the Korean churches and those of other denominations in what she calls the Pan Asian Faith Community of Southern California with some five thousand congregations nationwide. "We are leveraging the power base of churches to be more active in broad economic issues of jobs and housing, help with homelessness and other issues from immigration to youth and family problems," Im says.

And the KCCD has had more than two hundred partners contributing funds and expertise, ranging from large corporations to committees and institutions of the White House in Washington. The Korean Churches Organization has helped more than seven thousand homebuyers qualify for a total of $1.5 million in down payment assistance, and it has saved homeowners from foreclosures on housing worth $83 million in times of recession and other financial problems.

"If you lead without a political voice, you can leverage what you receive," she says and then recalls the Korean community's suffering that drove her ambitions. "Not long after the Los Angeles riots, when we were kicked down and crying with no one around to cry with us, I saw that if we became partners with the greater community it could increase our impact." She has worked with Jewish and Muslim organizations for community services and social justice. And over a decade and a half, Hyepin has broadened the work of community development to help with problems of juvenile delinquency, family strife, and education for people of all races.

She laughs to recall a time when she worked on a domestic violence study for a health and marriage initiative at Los Angeles City Hall. A leader of the committee suggested the research was primarily for the Latino and black communities and that Asian communities had no need of such help. Im scoffed and told the committee: "Model minorities don't exist. Asian fathers may not cry or show suffering openly, but we are all human. Working seventeen hours a day in convenience stores, saving to send kids to college, can wear people down."

Im's work has brought her to the White House several times for forums and she is a U.S. presidential appointee on the Board of the Corporation for National and Community Service. Significantly also, KCCD has received $5 million in grants from the Department of Labor for education of underprivileged people who want to increase their employment prospects by acquiring skills in modern technology. This year it will graduate its seventeenth class from the New Internet Users Technology Initiative.

In 2016–2017, Hyepin's activism paid off in affordable housing. KCCD succeeded in getting a new apartment building with a hundred units of reasonable-rent apartments added to a luxury development being built at Sixth Street and Vermont Avenue in Koreatown. Hyepin and her organization worked four years, campaigning with L.A. County Supervisor Mark Ridley-Thomas among others, to get the builder of the Meridian Apartment project to add a separate structure for affordable housing. The *Los Angeles Times* reported that the apartments, from studio to three-bedroom units, are available to families earning between $17,000 and $61,000 a year. They pay $560 a month for a two-bedroom apartment with on-site social services and after-school activities. Plus they have a transit pass for the Metroline that has a station half a block away. Thus, Los Angeles' Koreatown is becoming a more traditional center city. "The Korean community has a lot to offer this country," says Hyepin. "We just want to be on the same level at the decision-making table."

Her main efforts in 2017 have included the "SAIGU Campaign" to commemorate the twenty-fifth anniversary of the 1992 Los Angeles Riots. The campaign's purpose is to advocate and inspire unity. "Twenty-five years ago our city was torn and divided by the Riots," Hyepin said in a dinner speech heralding the Sa-I-Gu campaign. "Today they are many signs of progress that we can point to that has unified Los Angeles, the most diverse city in the United States, which is the most diverse country in the world." At a gala dinner for that campaign, Im's leadership had endorsements from U.S. Congress members in the Pan-Asian, Latino, and African American communities across the nation.

The endorsements underlined the fact that Los Angeles has changed enormously in the quarter century since the riots. Then it still resembled socially a "black-white" city. Racial disputes mainly concerned issues between the African American and traditional European-descendant "white" communities. Yes, there were disputes also with the growing populations of immigrants from Mexico and Central America, and of course there were resentments of the Korean shopkeepers. Those animosities were the kindling that ignited in the riots. But in the decades since then, Southern California has welcomed varieties of people from Southeast and Central Asia, from the broad Middle East and Eastern Europe, as well as Central and South America. And the region has seen billions of dollars of investment from across the world, new homes and developments throughout the area, and lately gigantic commercial real estate development in downtown Los Angeles. Of particular note are Chinese real estate companies building office and residential centers with entertainment, shopping, and restaurant venues. Los Angeles now welcomes forty-seven million tourists a year, including more than seven million residents from abroad. The region's universities continue to expand their facilities and global reach.

And yet, even as Hyepin Im and committees of Korean Americans planned the celebration in April 2017, she was in fear that once again the world could be turning upside down. Im and others saw young Koreans with visas to study or work in California and other areas worried about their ability in the future to come and go easily from the United States to Korea and back again. Indeed their worries were confirmed by news out of Washington that the State Department had ordered all U.S. embassies to be much tougher in reviewing all visa applications. Longer-term prospects for international work were now in question. And at one level, unexpected but filled with irony, Im reports, "Many Korean businesses are impacted by the deportation activities because many of their Hispanic customers are no longer turning out. Some say their businesses have decreased by 50 percent.

"I know as a Korean American who is a U.S. citizen," Im says with some anger. "I feel less safe with the environment of hate and discrimination being unleashed and the assaults of girls including Asian Americans. I am nervous not knowing when the next policy or tweet will attack the Asian American community."

As she put together events in 2017, Im strove to emphasize the Korean community's broader reach. The Korean Churches for Community Development Organization was renamed Faith and Community Empowerment, or FACE, in April that year. The name change was warranted given the variety of community organizations the Korean Churches group is now linked with, including the Afro Chamber of Commerce L.A., the National Association of Women Business Owners, Project Islamic H.O.P.E., and Advance Latino Inc.

Then, at a commemoration ceremony on April 29, 2017, at the vast Oriental Mission Church in Koreatown, Im declared a commitment for the Korean and all other communities to "Rebuild the American Dream Together." The letters of Sa-I-Gu, emblematic of the riots of 1992, are now made into an acronym to stand for "Serve Advocate Inspire Give Unite." Singers and musicians of many races sang "We Shall Overcome" in English and Korean—aided by translations shown on big screens. Political leaders—including former L.A. mayor Antonio Villaraigosa, California treasurer John Chiang, and L.A. city councilman David Ryu—came forth to praise heroic individuals who helped heal and unite communities after the riots and to look forward in faith and hope. And in a three-day summit in November of forums on jobs, housing, health, and other priorities, Los Angeles city council president Herb Wesson called out Im for her work with the L.A. Human Relations Commission to build trust among the city's many diverse communities.

Thus Los Angeles is growing from a relative adolescent to a modern metropolis on a par with New York and London, Shanghai and Seoul. It is imbued with the kind of vision that led Koreans to see L.A. and California as a new home in America and to sustain them after the shock of the riots, not to retreat into silence as Asian people were forced to do in previous centuries. The Korean and the Pan-Asian Communities know that exclusion from America and American life was the burden their ancestors fought to overcome. So it is a good bet that they will not shrink from the challenge now. Rather, the jolt of the riots has spurred Korean Americans to contribute new visions and leadership for California and the western U.S. that looks not eastward to the Atlantic Coast but westward toward the larger and wider Pacific World. It is a global and epochal shift.

This chapter should not close without recalling the thoughts of K. W. Lee, written two decades after the Riots, in which he pondered once more the suffering of mom-and-pop storekeepers in terms of the near biblical diaspora of the Jewish people who left Russia and Eastern Europe to escape pogroms in the nineteenth century.[24] "At risk of being presumptuous or overly romantic," Lee wrote, "I'm tempted to envision the beginning of a tribe of the latter-day Diaspora wandering this vast continent—the Koreans. It matters little that our (journey) is only a century old. What matters is that it's a biblical journey in so many ways."[25]

And then, K. W. Lee takes off: "Maybe God has chosen us to suffer—to redeem ourselves. He knew our collective wretchedness—almost pathological divisiveness, stubborn individualism, gleeful indifference to civil rules and common goals and ancient curse of self-loathing and mutual distrust—so He endowed us with a gift for our survival on earth: that Koreans-never-give-up spirit called Stamina."[26]

Yes, rhetoric warms the heart—but action rallies the spirit. Chapter 5 will tell of a good number of Korean American entrepreneurial firms that are innovating and inspiring new generations in the American economy.

CHAPTER 5

Entrepreneurial Energy and Deep Faith

Korean American businesses are driven by good old entrepreneurial spirit—the Horatio Alger tradition—but also by something more, a charitable reaching out that is openly religious in some cases, forthright and secular in others. It is a spirit of helping one's fellows in business and beyond in the broad American community.

There are many variations of that spirit among a dozen individuals and companies in this chapter. (Note: names of the entrepreneurs are boldfaced in this chapter.) Most of them are not very well known, but they all teach lessons in their various ways. Succeeding chapters will tell of rising ambitions among Korean community leaders as well as large Korean corporations that have risen to global prominence in the seventy years the U.S. government—particularly its military—has been involved in South Korea. All these chapters contain signposts to the future of the Korean community's investment in the American mosaic.

Let's begin with a man who recognized that customers prefer the brightly colored and new to the hush and reverence of tradition. Phillip Chang of Yogurtland adapted.[1] Devout like many Korean immigrants, Chang has ideas about management. He came to Los Angeles in 1985 when he was twenty-one. "We came, four of us in family, because my father needed medical care he could not get in Korea," Chang says today. "We had $3,000 at that time. I worked at two and three jobs."

It was not menial labor. He worked as a computer programmer and systems analyst for several companies. "When I came to America, I said when I am thirty years old I will have $1 million," Chang says. "Actually, when I turned thirty, I was $50,000 in credit card debt, and I had lost my business. I had to pay back all I could before I could start another business. But that's okay; you are an entrepreneur if you stand up more than fall."

And he did start again. In 2001, Chang founded Boba Loca, a shop in Koreatown serving the sweet milky tea with tapioca balls that originated in Taiwan. But Chang adapted the boba shop. "I noticed that in Chinese tea shops there were Chinese letters and decor. Customers didn't know what to order," he says. "But I looked at Starbucks and Jamba Juice and adapted to American mainstream. I made our Boba Loca stores bright and colorful, only English on the menus." It was a success. He sold thirty-three Boba Loca franchises in the next five years—and owned eight of them himself. "Koreans are always fast to buy franchises; cost of entry only $150,000 or so," Chang explains, referring to Korean communities' practice of pooling money to invest in business ownership.

In 2006 he sold Boba Loca because in its shop in Fullerton he had introduced a frozen yogurt product that customers served themselves from machines by pulling a lever to fill cups with yogurt, in sixteen flavors. They could add from thirty-three toppings of candies, fruit, and nuts and pay thirty cents per ounce at checkout counters. That first Yogurtland—"bright colors and polka dots, very mainstream," says Chang today—was near California State University, Fullerton and it was an immediate success. Within five years there were 150 franchised Yogurtlands and there are 331 today, including 36 international outlets in Mexico, Venezuela, Japan, Australia, Thailand, and Dubai.

This has made Yogurtland a large and profitable company that owns its headquarters building in Irvine and a yogurt factory nearby in Lake Forest. The parent company has about 250 employees. Success has made Chang a wealthy man, but financial success is but one tool of a successful business, he says. "We live in a two-bedroom condominium. Our daughter Claire, who is seventeen, asks 'why don't we buy a bigger house?' Well, yes, we could buy a house of $10 million or $20 million," Chang says. But what Chang has done instead is go on Christian missions, to South America and South Asia, bringing clean water to a village in one place, building school dormitories in another.

Then in 2013, after hiring and training a new chief executive, Chang stepped away from active management in Yogurtland to "devote my life to missionary work." But he came back in 2015 and resumed CEO duties. "I think in that time, the cooperative team culture I had built was going away, there was finger-pointing and gossip," Chang explains. He was hearing from former colleagues at Yogurtland, he says. "I feared the company would lose identity, and if you lose identity there is nothing left." So he decided "my calling is in business. I can run the company that I started and send people to missions, rather than go myself."

The pertinent point about Chang's travails—what others may call a midlife crisis—is that his religious work is the basis for his beliefs about business management. "I think it's important to look at a company as family members," he says. When he hires people for his company, he does not look first for technical skills. "I ask their ultimate goal in life. It probably will be some ideal for their family," Chang says. "Fine, if their work for our company can help them achieve such a goal, they will be better motivated than by financial gains." Ultimately, Chang explains, he is talking about "servant leadership—the image of Jesus washing the feet of others. These days MBAS talk about servant leadership in classes at business schools, but Christians know it from two thousand years ago." Chang, who is fifty-one years old, looks to pursue "my value as a servant" until he is seventy.

Such thoughts reflect teachings of American Protestant missionaries in the nineteenth century and Catholic Jesuits in the prior century, which Koreans have added to Buddhist and Confucian philosophies to make their country unique in Asia for the number of its people—30 percent of the total—following Western Christian religious thought and often broader perspectives. Chang, for example, looks at today's younger generations of Korean Americans and admires the way they have "a larger view that unites America and rising China and Korea to work together in this world. It is very strong."

Another example of such spirit is a contemporary fashion designer, Stella Lim of Ryu Fashion.[2] Stella Lim was already successful as a fashion designer in Seoul when she decided to come to Los Angeles in 2007 and open her brand-name Ryu Fashion in the teeming garment district. "There are 2,500 designers working in this market," Lim says, speaking through an interpreter in an interview for this book. "Yet it is easier than in Seoul," she adds, "because the market in Korea is different. Women in Korea are very aware about how they appear to people important to them, how they appear in another person's eyes. They want to dress up and be made up even when going out for a walk. So they prefer higher-end clothing—when other people see it they want to show."

American women are often fashion conscious too, she concedes, "but in America people wear what they want a lot of the time." And that suits Ryu Fashions, which designs clothing for young women, light, airy, attractive, and moderately priced—"at comparable quality and comparable prices," Lim adds. She studied design at Hongik University in Seoul, the leading fashion and art school in Korea. She later took a second degree in marketing.

The U.S. market also is much larger than Korea's, and that gives Ryu more variety in pricing. Operating now out of its own warehouse and showrooms in Broadway Place near downtown L.A., Ryu has grown in less than a decade to twenty-five employees, including five other designers, and "just under $20 million in sales," Lim says. The company operates what it calls "foreign sourcing infrastructure for production," which means designs are created at Ryu's L.A. headquarters and beamed to China, where the clothes are manufactured. Garments are then shipped back to Los Angeles and packed for sending to small- to medium-sized retail companies around the country by United Parcel Service. Lim and her staff gather wholesale customers by traveling to trade shows in Las Vegas, Atlanta, Dallas, New York, and San Francisco. Or buyers visit Lim and her partner Chris Jeong, head of marketing, at a conference room at Ryu's warehouse and showrooms.

It is the conference room, with one wall covered with photographs of children from many countries, that reveals another side to Stella Lim and Ryu's business. In addition to the children's pictures is a verse from Corinthians 9:8, St. Paul's epistle to the people of ancient Corinth, which says, "And God is able to make all grace abound to you so that in all things you have sufficiency and you will abound in every good work." The meaning is you will have enough, so share with others.

The verse is on the wall because from the start Ryu contributed from its profits to help children in poor countries. "We started with one child and now support 150 children with the profits, giving through World Vision"—an organization that is not really a church but is religious, the designer explains. World Vision began in postwar China, when Rev. Bob Pierce, a Baptist missionary from Los Angeles, was asked by a nurse to help a poor orphan. He gave a little money and promised to keep doing so. In the process, he organized World Vision, which made a major push in the early 1950s in Korea, where hundreds of thousands of orphans roamed the streets of Seoul and other cities during and after the Korean War. World Vision in those early days helped to organize adoptions of Korean orphans by American adoptive parents, a task later taken over by Korean government agencies. World Vision, now based in Monrovia, in L.A. County, operates today in more than a hundred countries.

Lim's company donations are "to help all children," she says. Her vision is broad: "All children have opportunity and a little bit of skill but cannot show (develop) it because they are poor and the environment of their countries is poor. We want to do something, to share some of (our profits) to help other children and families."

Korea's Religious Culture

Such stories grace this book not to talk about religion as such but to portray the Korean community, whose people often talk about their own motivations and culture in religious terms. The modern history of the Korean homeland has a lot to do with that. "The impact of Christianity in modern Korea is unique," wrote Frank Gibney in his history tome *Korea's Quiet Revolution: From Garrison State to Democracy*, published twenty-five years ago.[3] The history of that Western religion "is far older in both China and Japan, but in neither country has it played a significant modern role. In Korea, however, Christian thinking has entered the national bloodstream," Gibney wrote.[4]

Here the strongest influence has been Protestant and American. The first Protestant missionary, Dr. Horace Allen, a medical missionary, arrived in 1884. Others followed him and established schools and hospitals, ultimately founding Yonsei University and Ewha Womans (CQ) University,[5] which dates to 1886 and is today the world's largest female educational institution. "It was during the Japanese colonial period that the Americans began to make converts in the mass, partly because to be Christian was one way to get a non-Japanese international education—and to demonstrate independence from Japanese rules," Gibney said.

And there was another very important aspect to Korean society's ready embrace of the Christian faith and Western way of thinking. Koreans could read because they had a written language called Hangeul devised for easy literacy. In the year 1446, a phonetic alphabet called Hangeul was invented to help the lower class and women read in some fashion because most people had difficulty learning the characters of the Chinese-based language read by the aristocratic and leading classes.[6] So Hangeul was invented but then banned from "polite" society as an "inferior" language for some four and a half centuries. But Christian missionaries found that using Hangeul helped them to communicate with the common people. So they translated their Bible into Hangeul and translated their other literature into that writing form as well.

This not only earned respectability for the common language, but it made Korea one of the most literate nations on earth. "Whereas in China and India one among a thousand can read," wrote American missionary

James Gale in 1909, "in Korea reading is almost universal." The long-term effect has been incalculable and historic for the Korean people.

"Christians played prominent roles in Korea's independence movement, and the importance given to women's education led to many female students joining that movement in the colonial period," Gibney reported. "And the emphasis on individual responsibility, stressing democracy and equality, has continued in Korea leading to formation of labor unions and a tradition of protest movements."[7]

In recent times, the Urban Industrial Mission, a Christian-led organization, made Korean workers aware of their rights in the fifties and sixties. And in the seventies and eighties, a women's union was formed and led by Methodist minister Rev. Cho Hwa-sun, who was jailed by the dictatorial government of that time, wrote Bruce Cumings in *Korea's Place in the Sun, a Modern History*, published in 1997 and then again in an updated edition in 2005.[8] But labor union activity along with a shift to more progressive thinking among many business leaders helped ultimately to turn South Korea toward democracy in the late 1980s.

Indeed, "there is a strong correlation between the open-minded thinking of the Christian religion and the ranks of business leaders in Korea and the Korean American community in the U.S.," says Professor Richard Drobnick, founding director of the International Business Education and Research program at USC.[9]

Stories of two entrepreneurs reflect those spirits—one asserting that her success in the United States has been possible because she is free of class system restrictions in the old country, and the other a now-renowned chef reflecting a spirit that is rebellious yet devoted to helping the less fortunate among the diverse peoples of Los Angeles.

Sabrina Kay, California Design College, Fremont College

Dr. Sabrina Kay's resume is impressive: chief executive of Fremont College, founder twenty-three years ago of California Design College, which she sold.[10] She has a doctorate from Wharton in work-based learning, a master's in education from the University of Pennsylvania, and a master's in business administration from USC.

The life story behind those credentials is even more interesting and speaks volumes about Korean immigrants' passions for education, business, religion, and sense of mission. Kay came to Los Angeles in 1983 with her parents, who opened an apparel store in Santa Ana. She was eighteen and enrolled at Cal State Long Beach wanting to study fashion. But life took a turn; she became pregnant and bore a daughter.

"When I became pregnant in college I thought my life was over. My life would have been over in Korea," Kay says today. "But because I was in America, it made me grow up very fast and able to focus."[11]

She continued to study designing at Los Angeles' Fashion Institute of Design and Merchandising, where she saw that knowledge of computer-aided design was becoming a needed skill for workers in the fashion industry. So she decided to open a school to teach those skills. In 1991 she opened California Design College with $500,000 borrowed from her father. In a Korean-owned building on Wilshire Boulevard, she taught Korean students CAD/CAM (computer-aided design/computer-aided manufacturing) skills. The tuition was $12,000 a year, for which students could get federal grants for job training. "I wanted to establish a technical school that would teach job skills without all the other academic courses," Kay later recalled. She worked hard and made a success of the school, and in 2003 she sold Design College for $15 million to Education Management Corp., a Pittsburgh-based company. The school continues today as Art Institute of California–Hollywood.

Kay, however, didn't retire at thirty-eight, nor buy a yacht or a mansion. She went to USC for an MBA degree, but still she had questions of a different kind. "I needed to find my purpose of existence," Kay says. "There had to be a reason why I had business success early in my life; some kind of God's purpose. I felt really blessed and did not know what to do with my money." So she followed up by earning a doctorate at the University of Pennsylvania's Wharton School. It was in her first week at Wharton, she says today, that she found her mission. "The first week I remember how impressed I was with my colleagues and professors. Coming into class I felt I grew an inch every day. But of course, they were people from middle and upper classes who had all gone to good schools. And it hit me that good education is what makes the difference in every society."

So her first weekend home from Wharton she bought Fremont College, a for-profit business school that dates to 1879 as Platt College in St. Joseph, Missouri, and to 1986 in Los Angeles. By 2007, armed with her doctorate and a plan for what she terms "professional action learning," Kay took command at Fremont.

Professional action learning is based on preparing students for a specific line of work. Thus, what law firms require in training for their paralegals' Fremont's course will teach them through lectures, practice sessions, and so on. Similarly, what health clinics and medical offices demand in training for therapists and office managers Fremont teaches

Friendship and Peace Bell, at Good Samaritan
Hospital, L.A., donated by Severance Hospital and
Yonsei University, Seoul. Photo by Patricia Flanigan.

in courses of study that run fifteen months for accredited bachelor's and
associate degrees. Her idea, Kay explains, is to give working people who
had "good education," a chance to qualify for better jobs. As she worked
with mostly Korean garment workers in the 1990s, she is doing similar
training with about 360 mostly non-Korean students at Fremont. There
is a difference in that California Design was a virtual one-woman shop
while Fremont, with tuition of $33,000 a year, is a larger company with
a board of directors led by financial executive Frank Baxter, former CEO
of Jefferies & Co. and U.S. ambassador to Uruguay from 2006 to 2009.
Sabrina Kay is chancellor and chief executive.

She also is heavily involved in charitable work as chair of the After-
School All Stars, a youth organization founded by former governor
Arnold Schwarzenegger, and in the Korean American Coalition and
the Council of Korean Americans.

"I think my second career is to give opportunity back to America which gave me opportunity," Kay says. And then she turns up the
volume: "There is no country like America that gives opportunity to
almost anybody without social connections or ranking systems," she

declares. "You don't have to be born into an upper class to succeed. This country gives opportunity to everybody and anybody. There is no other country like this."

In thinking about Korean culture and that of America, Kay recalls her high school in Seoul, where marks were posted monthly in ranks of 1 to 1200. "Every month you risked public humiliation," she says, "and if my brothers and I came in number 5, my mother would ask why there were four ahead of us. My parents took out mortgages to pay for after-school programs—tennis and violin lessons. They were university graduates but came to America for better schools for their children."

She recalls her daughter, now in her late twenties, when she was younger, having grown up with Kay's parents. "It was so interesting. When we would talk English, she would argue with me. But when we would speak Korean, she would become obedient."

Finally, Kay says of Korean Americans, "I think how much has improved, how much we have integrated proudly to this society. I see a lot of young Korean Americans who want political office to have a seat at the table where decisions are going to be made. I am very proud to be Korean American."

Roy Choi, Master Chef

"It was about 4 inches in diameter, one and a half bites at most," wrote Roy Choi of his Korean Mexican taco. "Filled with meat that had been chopped all day then sizzled to a crusty niblet of life, then showered with chopped onions and cilantro, lime juice everywhere, salsa roja, smoky and pungent—there it was, Los Angeles on a plate."[12] Choi created that niblet in 2008 and sold it on the streets from his first food truck, called Kogi. Choi was thirty-eight years old when he triumphed with the Kogi idea. Today he has eight restaurants in Los Angeles and more opening all the time. He has become the California face of Korean cooking.

Yet he and L.A. are not alone. Korean restaurants were estimated to be a $5 billion industry in 2017 by a market research firm that counted 6,482 outlets nationwide. Notable examples include Judy Joo, host of *Korean Food Made Simple* on TV's Cooking Channel.[13] Judy learned recipes watching her Korean mother cook authentic dishes in her New York home. But she did not initially choose a culinary career. Rather, she traded fixed-income securities at Morgan Stanley, following a degree in engineering at Columbia University. But she quit that and went to live in London, where she serves Korean dishes at her own restaurant.

Another example is the Mandu Restaurant in Washington, DC, owned and run by Danny Lee and his mother, Yesoon Lee.[14] Mandu means dumpling in Korean and the restaurant serves a variety of dishes, including pork dumplings with ginger and garlic and rice cakes with savory, sweet, and spicy gochujang, or red chili pepper paste. The Lees also hold monthly chef collaborations to educate guests on the nuances of Korean food. Danny Lee says his mission is to "elevate Korean cuisine to top ranks across the nation and the world."

But for blending flavors of old country and new, Roy Choi's life story embodies many characteristics—unpredictable, rebellious, and innovative—of Los Angeles and its Korean community. He was born in Seoul in 1970 and had a cleft palate, which the doctor sewed up immediately. His parents, Soo Myung Choi and Yuon-jin Choi, returned with him in 1972 to Los Angeles, where both had lived briefly in the 1960s. They worked at several businesses. Choi's mother, an excellent cook, was so good at making kimchi, the pickled fermented cabbage that is a staple of the Korean diet, that she made a business of selling it door to door. The Chois opened a restaurant in Anaheim called Silver Garden when Roy Choi was seven. It succeeded until the neighborhood declined, and they moved on. Eventually, through relatives, they got into the jewelry business and made a comfortable living.

But teenage Roy got in with a gang in Buena Park, and his parents sent him to military school in Signal Hill. He went on to college at Cal State Fullerton, graduated, and got jobs in financial services. But he developed a gambling addiction. His father dragged him from a card club one night, and he straightened out but started drinking heavily and went downhill again. Finally a friend urged him to try cooking, which he studied at local schools until his parents sent him to the Culinary Institute of America in Hyde Park, New York. That proved a turning point. He came back to L.A. and worked his way up to a lead chef at the Beverly Hilton Hotel. Then restaurateur David Overton invited him to work at Rock Sugar, an elaborate new restaurant in Century City devoted to Asian cuisines: Thai, Vietnamese, Japanese, Chinese, Korean. Choi succeeded in his training until he had what amounts to a nervous breakdown—as he wrote in his book *L.A. Son* in 2013: "What was once second nature became foreign to me. I fell behind; I couldn't tell my cooks who needed what, when and where. Recipes seemed to disappear inside my head."[15] He redoubled his work effort but to no avail, and after three months was fired.

It was at that point, with Mark Munguera, a buddy from the Hilton, he developed the Korean Mexican taco for the Kogi truck and remade his life. Now at forty-eight, with a growing family and hailed as one of America's finest chefs, Choi is turning to charitable work—training youngsters in poor neighborhoods for jobs in food preparation and also pioneering healthier ingredients in the foods those youngsters eat. He and chef Daniel Patterson have opened a new restaurant called LocoL in Watts that emphasizes well-made and healthy burgers, chicken sandwiches, and other specialties at low prices. Choi has said he is on a mission to improve the diets and lives of poorer folks and also to train youngsters to be chefs and restaurant operators. "We believe that chefs should feed America and not suits," he says.[16] "I'd really love to see the chefs.... Go to the poorest points of their neighborhoods and think about.... food in the schools, in the neighborhoods, in the prisons, and think about how to bring some more affordable food there."[17]

Choi and Patterson have opened a LocoL in Oakland and are planning for other low-income neighborhoods, where, Choi says, they hope "to provide skill sets so our staff can move on in a craft or career within Locol or beyond."[18]

So, what lies ahead for Korean food and its growing popularity? Simple, Korean barbecue, which is called bulgogi, or "fire meat," and kimchi, the fermented cabbage that goes back millennia in Korea, will take their place alongside Szechuan, Hunan, and Cantonese cuisines from China; sushi and teriyaki from Japan; Pad Thai; Vietnamese Pho—not to mention pizza, corned beef, and bratwurst in this country where choices abound.

Let us now read stories of sons and daughters of Korean immigrants who are building businesses on foundations of their forebears and inspiring new generations of Korean Americans. First look at a company based in Vernon that gathers fish from around the world and brings food to markets and restaurants of the Los Angeles region. Then look at a woman from war-torn Korea who built a financial business by creating her own credit system to lend to small garment makers and shopkeepers.

The Huh Family, Pacific American Fish Co.

Peter Huh recalls his father, Joseph, as an entrepreneur from the start back in U.S.-occupied Korea.[19] "My father had a pretty interesting business in Korea with the U.S. military. He took all their trash out. The military during that time was very wasteful. Everything came in crates from the U.S., stuff for the post exchanges and the canteens. My father would go in and demolish all the cardboard boxes, and he would recycle all the stuff they were throwing away, cans and bottles and many other things and he would make money from the trash."

"He came here in 1970 and did not speak the language. But seeing opportunity in a new country, he wanted to do something he loved, and he loved the fish in the seas and in the Korean diet. So out of the blue, he said he was going to be in the fish business," Peter Huh recalls. Joseph got a job in a Koreatown supermarket working in the fish department, rose early to go to the fish markets near Stanford Avenue in downtown L.A. to secure fresh seafood for the store. "He never got paid for overtime but became a manager," says his son. Joseph ultimately opened Pacific American Fish Co. in 1977 in Vernon to become a wholesale supplier of fish to restaurants and markets.

Peter Huh worked at the company as a teenager before going to Amherst University in the early 1980s. He took semesters and whole years off from college to come back and help the business and ultimately graduated in 1985 with a degree in chemistry. Joseph Huh died in 1992 at the age of sixty-three. Over the last twenty-five years, Peter as chairman along with his younger brother Paul, vice president of sales, and Peter's wife, Jihee, as vice president for new venture development, have led the growth of Pacific American Fish (Pafco). It has become a large company that gets fish from fishing vessels and seafood farms in North and South America and Asia. It processes millions of pounds of seafood every week at a giant plant in Vernon, where 250 employees move fresh fish for Costco Wholesale and other large grocers and also prepare ready-to-cook and ready-to-eat varieties for restaurants and homes. With annual revenues of more than $300 million, Pafco has operations in China, Vietnam, Thailand, Chile, Peru, Boston, and San Francisco.

"How did we build the business?" Peter asks rhetorically. In classic entrepreneurial parlance, they found needs and filled them. "The Korean American community really didn't have a reliable supplier of seafood, and that gave us an opportunity," he explains. "And the Chinese community, here for so long, did not have its own wholesale supplier of seafood, so we filled that vacuum. Those two communities have been our bedrock, and we expanded to the Filipino American community and some of the Middle Eastern supermarkets and restaurants." In diversity is strength, in other words. "The Chinese community has been so helpful, telling us to go find this fish or that. We have suppliers and a manufacturing joint venture there in Tianjin, a friend of my father's. We've been working with them for thirty years."

Moreover, the company is an innovator. In a breakthrough two years ago, in cooperation with farms in South Korea and the Korean government, Pafco constructed tanks that allow fish to swim live in Hanjin containers as they cross the ocean, thus delivering very fresh flounder and black rockfish. Under Pafco's Pete's Seafood division, run by Jihee Huh, dinners and delicacies can be ordered online and delivered. Pacific American has begun distribution through Amazon.

Bravo, in a word. The family and Pacific American Fish are another example of hardworking Koreans improving the economy and broadening the vision of Los Angeles and America. But there's more. The Huh family in turn has taken up the American tradition of "giving back" and changing lives. Peter recalls: "When my father was an immigrant here, I went to Amherst on a scholarship created by someone before my time. That scholarship paid my way to go there. I wanted to give back and pay forward for the next generation." So he established a scholarship for Asian Studies at Amherst. "I don't care who receives the scholarship," Peter Huh says. "It encourages interest in Asia."

Jihee Huh, a Korean American, grew up in New York City. "My father came with $50 to the 1962 World's Fair in New York," she says. "He opened a wig shop on Broadway in Manhattan, one of the first Koreans to have a store there." Jihee learned to play flute at the Manhattan School of Music Precollege Division and then graduated from St. John's University. She has been heavily involved in philanthropy. She served as trustee for Asians United for Self Empowerment—which has advocated for Korean women. Jihee worked to get the U.S. Congress to pass a resolution urging Japan to do more to make amends to Korean women abused as sex slaves—Comfort Women—for Japan's military during World War II. She has a commendation from Congress for work on that cause. She is also a trustee for Children's Hospital Los Angeles and served as chairwoman of Southern California Public Radio, Station KPCC.

The Huhs' efforts are remarked upon because most immigrant groups have taken several generations before adopting charitable giving beyond one's own people. Korean Americans appear to be moving a bit faster. "Our generation is a bit more active," Peter Huh says. "We grew up here, and we can provide for ourselves but also think more broadly about the local community." To that point, Peter and Jihee—and Paul Huh also—are working through Chadwick School in Palos Verdes to support a new school in Songdo, a model city and community being built near Incheon, Korea. "We want to provide kids the freedom and opportunity to learn," says Jihee. "And we want to bring art and music to Korean schools," Peter adds, "as we bring the same to schools here in Los Angeles."

The Huhs worked to help David Ryu get elected to the Los Angeles City Council in 2015. "Some friends were reluctant," Jihee says. "They would say, 'he hasn't a chance; he's not going to make it.' But I would answer 'if we don't try, how will anybody make it?,'" Ryu won a runoff election for the City Council seat. (See chapter 7 for more on Councilman Ryu.) The Huhs also are involved in the Korean community's effort to increase Korean community participation in national politics.

Sunnie S. Kim, Hana Financial

Kim founded Hana Financial Inc. in 1994, because she wanted to lend to the small family-owned businesses that most banks—even Korean banks—viewed as financial risks.[20] "But I understood their potential and wanted to help these family businesses," she says. So she founded Hana as a company that could help garment industry clothing makers and small designer shops by using factoring—a form of finance in which the lender forwards money to the manufacturers or small designers so they don't have to wait 30 to 120 days to be paid for their shipments. The lender takes over that waiting period, charging a percentage of the total amount and facilitating the flow of business.

Hana made a success of the factoring business ultimately, but it was not easy. There was little capital around, she explains, and many garment makers supported those who sold clothing to retail chains, such as Forever 21, by supplying them at risk of their own meager capital and companies. Her Hana Financial helped some apparel firms on her own judgment—thus her remark that "I loaned money to Don Chang (founder of Forever 21) when banks wouldn't look at him."

But Sunnie Kim did more. She moved her lending into the realm of small mom-and-pop grocery stores and dry-cleaning family businesses that no American bank or finance company—and even fewer Korean banks—would readily lend to. "We created our own credit system for those thinly capitalized companies," Sunnie explains. "Where most banks would look at a family with children and count the kids as costs or liabilities, we would see them as labor to help the family business," she says. Hana's "credit system" thus helped many small Korean businesses to survive lean times or capital perils that threaten any small company.

What Sunnie calls her own credit system is actually a much older tradition, a throwback to such businesspeople as A. P. Giannini, founder of the Bank of America, who knew his Italian fishermen off San Francisco were good credit risks when other banks shunned them. Sunnie Kim and Hana, in effect, were lending on judgment of the people and families borrowing rather than abstract mathematical formulas. "I wanted to be a lender to small family business because I admired GE Capital and its leader, Jack Welch, although I did not know him personally," Sunnie says. However, her office in downtown L.A. holds a photograph of herself and Jack Welch.

Sunnie Kim was well grounded in banking and finance well before starting Hana Financial. She grew up in Korea and graduated from Ewha Womans (CQ) University in Seoul in the late sixties, when the country was still very poor. She went to work at the government-owned Korea Exchange Bank, where, she recalls, "we had no system and little equipment; we counted money by hand." In 1974 she came to Los Angeles along with six sisters and brothers and continued working for the Exchange Bank's California branch.

Then with other Korean colleagues she cofounded Hanmi Bank in Los Angeles in 1984 and followed by cofounding Center Bank in 1988. Those banks received a flow of money from Korea in the 1980s and after to invest in real estate. She started Hana Financial in 1994 with three employees and did not take a salary for herself for the first year and more. The company now is twenty-two years old and prosperous, doing more than $2 billion a year in traditional factoring and other kinds of finance with nine offices around the United States and "clients from all cultures and backgrounds," she says proudly.

She has broadened Hana's business by qualifying it for a U.S. Small Business Administration license, which means that the federal government guarantees 75 percent of some of its loans. She moved into mortgage banking in 2010, when housing markets were still devastated by recession. Sunnie's six sisters and brothers have done well, in finance and other fields. "One sister is an artist," she says, "and my brother has built a construction company." Of course, the Korean American community's economy has grown nationwide and far beyond the days of "thinly capitalized companies." In other words, Sunnie Kim has been a key lender to the growth of the Korean community's success in that regard—and to many other communities as well in the forty-two years she has been in Los Angeles.

She has received many honors: Entrepreneur of the Year in 2012, and an award from City of Hope hospital. In 2015, Sunnie was honored by apparel industry executives at a "Black & White Ball," which was held to benefit National Jewish Health, a Denver hospital. In a short speech, Sunnie recalled the Korea of her youth, when she brought rice to hungry people and taught reading to those who had no education. She complimented "National Jewish Health for its commitment to treat people who do not have the finances."

But she is not uncritical of her own Korean people, whom she challenges. "Koreans need to go outside their own circles; they are not very trusting of others," she exclaims. "But they should not fear to go outside their small community, to share knowledge with others. They are hardworking people but if they go outside and share more knowledge, they could be much better," says Sunnie Kim, a leading member of the "first or immigrant" generation of Korean Americans.

On to technology. The Korean community has an impressive number of innovators, entrepreneurs, and top executives in information and medical technology companies. Read of a few examples here, along with mentions of South Korea's advances in those high-tech fields.

John Suh, LegalZoom

A Baker Scholar from Harvard Business School, John Suh is president of LegalZoom, the company that through its website enables customers to create their own legal documents—for prenuptial agreements, divorces, wills, and other matters—and guides them in their use, sparing them heavy legal expenses. Before LegalZoom, which he has headed since 2007, Suh cofounded a company named Castling, which helped other firms to create Internet divisions, and then he ran Studio Direct, the Internet division of the Hong Kong–based global supply company Li and Fung.

Born in New York to Korean immigrant parents who are physicians—father an endocrinologist and mother a pediatrician—Suh went to Harvard College and then to its business school. "I wanted to be an entrepreneur," he says.[21] His parents on the other hand "always hoped I would go into medical research or perhaps law so that my brain could solve world problems." This, says Suh, reflects their Korean culture. "In Korea, social stature puts academics at the forefront, professors at the pinnacle, but entrepreneurs are put low." So when he continued to be fascinated with the technological breakthroughs made possible by computers, cell phones, and the Internet, his parents would suggest he was still "playing with toys."

Of course, that contrast only illustrates that ideas and values change from one generation to the next, especially when generations transition from old country to new. John Suh has many thoughts about such matters. In one conversation for this book, he explained the extraordinary drive of many Korean Americans as well as their devotion to collective help. "Korean culture is Confucian, hierarchical, and disciplined with a sense of obligation," Suh said. "When we came to this country, we found that American culture at its foundation is Puritan, the New England tradition of social commitment. The melding of these two cultures is very powerful. Young Korean Americans must figure out how to commit time and effort to help the community; more than money although money is important."

Yet at the same time, he is concerned that the oft-repeated emphasis on hard work and education makes only one story get told. "It's the old model minority myth," he says, but it means that many Korean Americans who have social and economic problems common to all communities—poverty, domestic strife, juvenile delinquency—get ignored or scorned. So Suh is a leading member of the Network of Korean American Leaders, or NetKAL, an organization formed at USC in 2005 through which successful Korean Americans help their fellows.

As to the Korean community in business, finance, and technology, however, the story has been progress over the fifty-odd years the Koreans have been here in large numbers. "It is still true that if you are born outside the United States, you are a hundred times more likely to start a business," Suh says. But it has become easier to do. "The first immigrants didn't have credit and had to pass around the hat to get small amounts. Now it's quite different. We have our own community banks and venture capital and angel funding, the full complement of capitalism is available."

At his own company, LegalZoom, Suh says he has raised $800 million from venture backers in his decade of leading the firm. LegalZoom was founded in 2001 by Brian Lee, a serial entrepreneur.[22] Born in Seoul, Brian Lee immigrated at the age of one with his parents to Huntington Beach. A magnum cum laude graduate from UCLA and Juris Doctor from its law school, Lee initially worked at the Skadden, Arps law firm but got an idea for do-it-yourself online processing of legal documents. He cofounded LegalZoom in 2001 with Robert Shapiro and two other lawyers. Then in 2009 he cofounded Shoe Dazzle with reality TV star Kim Kardashian. It is an e-commerce club that brings boutique shopping online by enrolling women for a $39 fee and sending them one stylish pair of shoes per month. And in 2011 Lee cofounded the Honest Company with actress Jessica Alba. The company makes eco-friendly, nontoxic products such as baby lotions and diapers and household products. Lee credits the "beauty and legacy of our Korean culture" as inspiration for his business career.

Korean immigrant techies also have flourished in Silicon Valley.

Michael Yang, Repeat Entrepreneur

Yang came to San Jose with his parents in 1976 at fourteen years of age.[23] "The family franchised a 7-11 store where everyone worked, including the children," Yang says. There was a family connection to an earlier technological time, as Michael's uncle K. Philip Hwang had developed computer terminals and founded TeleVideo Inc. in 1979. His uncle mentored Michael, who studied engineering and computer science at UC Berkeley and Columbia University in New York, before returning to San Jose to work at a pioneering information technology firm and then founding mySimon.com as a comparison shopping site in 1988 with Yeogirl Yun, another Korean immigrant entrepreneur. It became a success, Yang explains today, because its algorithms compared product quality and other features as well as prices. The company was sold to CNET in 2000 at the height of the dot.com boom for $700 million—much of it in CNET stock, which soon deflated in the dot.com bust. But Yang understood that the boom-bust cycle was "only the beginning of the online economy, whether shopping for food and products or for travel or even for healthcare," he said back then.

That was eighteen years ago, and now the online economy, the Internet, and artificial intelligence economy is growing every year. In 2017 online retail sales grew to $111 billion and accounted for 8.2 percent of the total—a new high for the year as has been the pattern for a decade. Yang understood the shift to online retail and in 2004 with Yeogirl Yun he founded Become.com, a comparison shopping website for the world's new approach to buying. It was successful, and Become.com was sold in 2014 to Connexity.com (formerly Shopzilla). Yang remains a director of the company and in 2017 started his own investment fund, Michael Yang Capital Management, to invest in fledgling public companies in the continuing shift in technology.

These few of many examples show that Korean Americans' high-tech abilities are not a flash in the pan but reflect a long legacy. South Korea, in the decades since 1960, has developed an advanced technological economy. In *Korea's Place in the Sun*, Bruce Cumings wrote of President Park Chung-hee's campaign begun in the sixties to have Korea produce all elements of an industrial economy, from machine tools to cars. One result of that effort: By 1980, South Korea (population then thirty-eight million) was producing more semiconductors than the allegedly mighty Soviet Union, population more than three hundred million at that time.[24]

And the beat goes on today, with investment money flowing two ways across the Pacific. Two quick references will drive the point home.[25] Eric Kim cofounded Goodwater Capital in 2014 in San Francisco. Kim, a Phi Beta Kappa and Magna Cum Laude graduate of Yale, with an MBA from Stanford, is a director of half a dozen startups in the United States and abroad. He cofounded Biomimedica, a medical device company that develops synthetic cartilage and related products for repair of knees and other joints. But more pertinent to our transpacific point, Kim is a director and early venture capital backer of Coupang, an e-commerce giant founded in 2010 in Seoul by Bom Suk Kim,[26] son of a Hyundai executive, who was brought to the United States at thirteen for prep school at Deerfield Academy, then went on to Harvard and Harvard Business School. But Bom Kim dropped out of the Business School to return to Seoul and create Coupang, the mobile marketing and delivery company that is being called the "Amazon of South Korea." The firm's Rocket Delivery system employs thirty-six hundred drivers to get goods to customers all over South Korea within twenty-four hours. Coupang has now been backed by global investment companies, including Black-Rock in the United States and SoftBank in Japan, and is estimated to be worth $5 billion. It now has offices and operations in Beijing, Los Angeles, Seattle, Shanghai, and Silicon Valley.

Next we will move on to chapter 6, which will tell of Korean communities on a national level, spreading their beliefs, lobbying Congress, and fighting for a "seat at the table" for future generations.

CHAPTER 6

"We Korean Americans can move this country forward"

Los Angeles is home not only to more Koreans than any city except Seoul but home also to the vision Korean Americans have for the country and society their parents immigrated to. Several Korean American organizations make that clear. The first, the Network of Korean American Leaders, was organized in 2005 at USC's Center for Asian Pacific Leadership. Much more than a social club, NetKAL is a boot camp for social activism among Korean American applicants who enroll for six weekends of training in ways to help the community. Their social mission is intended for the immigrants who have experienced discrimination or confusion about laws but also for people in need beyond the Korean community in all parts of the United States. Since 2006, NetKAL has trained more than two hundred graduates of its programs, young professionals in business, law, healthcare, and government offices at federal, state, and local levels.

The group was organized by Marilyn Flynn, dean of the USC School of Social Work, where the Center for Asian Pacific Leadership is housed. To head NetKAL, she reached back to Michigan State University, where she had taught, for Dr. Je Hoon Lee, a graduate of two universities in Seoul who earned a doctorate at Michigan State and led its outreach programs for international students.[1] He has led ten years of NetKAL classes and initiated annual summits in Los Angeles and San Francisco, New York, and Washington, DC, of Korean Americans involved in social causes, political action, and business innovation. "As the Korean American community in the U.S. matures," Lee said at the 2015 Summit in New York, "the landscape is shifting from issues of immigration to broader civic issues of family and child care, poverty and education and job training for the broader society." The organization now declares national days of service for the Korean community nationwide.

Enlarging the vision in 2016, Lee set up a NetKAL program in Seoul to create an international fellowship, recruiting local leaders from among the cities and regions of Korea. "Every year a delegation of NetKAL members travel to their homeland to connect with business, civic and government leaders," Lee wrote in his announcement. The new program, he said, will "strengthen existing ties and expand NetKAL's growing connections between the United States and Korea." Those connections were growing—with some complications, however—as events in 2017–2018 made profound changes in Korea and the United States.

The second organization, the Council of Korean Americans (CKA), was founded in 2011 by a small group meeting in Washington.[2] The new organization pledged at the outset to "be a voice for Koreans in the mainstream of U.S. society, lobbying on questions and policies." The CKA has grown now to a hundred leaders, an international network of members, and a record of three Summit Meetings at government levels in Washington. Michael Yang, the entrepreneur who started companies in Silicon Valley, helped to set CKA as a nonprofit 503c social welfare organization for tax purposes in 2011. He is also an early member of NetKAL at USC. "We needed to create a group independent of USC in order to work for political causes and lobby for change," Yang said in an interview.

Current chair of the CKA Board is Dr. June Lee, a research scientist and adjunct professor at the UC San Francisco School of Medicine.[3] At the 2017 Summit she said, "I think with this third summit, we have found a focus on what we need to do for the Korean community in the United States and in Korea's as well." At the Washington summit, CKA members had briefings at the Pentagon on U.S. policy toward North and South Korea and briefings at the U.S. Senate on how best to lobby Congress on political questions. Currently the council is lobbying for a shift in U.S. policy toward North Korea, and it has spoken out against White House moves to restrict immigration.

The CKA also is allied with Asian Americans Advancing Justice, created formally in 2013 by combining five organizations across the United States that have worked for civil rights and against discrimination since 1991.[4] The AAAJ has taught Asian immigrants how to become U.S. citizens, and protected Asian people from harassment and prejudicial actions by police and local governments. And in 2017 it stepped up its opposition to U.S. budget increases for federal-policing agencies that arrest and try to deport undocumented immigrants. "A waste of taxpayer money," the AAAJ called such budget requests. "Rather than separating families through mass deportation efforts, the U.S. government should spend more money on building infrastructure and creating economic opportunities," the AAAJ said in a formal statement sent to members of Congress.

Thus Korean Americans are becoming part of what they call "mainstream" American society. As they work on issues for their own people, they are realizing they must spread help to all people and communities. They are not strangers from another world but citizens of this city, this town, this America. It is a stage that all immigrant groups come to as succeeding generations adapt to America. Yet the Korean community, arriving at that stage sooner than others in the past, is proving a force for change.

Why should that be? A big reason is for their children. Many Korean Americans grew up experiencing prejudice, ignorance—being called "Chink" on the playground. Most have dealt with feelings of being the village outsider but wanting to make sure their own children are able to participate fully in American society—have "a seat at the table" as they invariably put it. To understand the journey, let us look at a few Korean Americans who have adapted to new lives and communities in their new country. Their stories reveal not only prejudice in the new world but lack of opportunity and cultural limits in the old.

A good person to start with is Esther Star Kimm, who is chief people officer at Stealth Mode Startup Company, her latest assignment in a twenty-year career as a corporate recruiter.[5] (Note: Boldface type will be used for profiles in this chapter as well.) Kimm grew up in Torrance in the 1970s, when, she says, other kids would ask, "What are you a Chink?" because they didn't know Korea. "So I would say, 'Yeah, whatever you think.'" Her parents had lived through the Korean War. "My mom came from a poor family but managed to work and study her way to Seoul University, the top school," Kimm says. "It took a long time because she had to flee south to Busan since she was at a tender age that was dangerous for a woman."

Her mother was working at the Korean Embassy in Taiwan when she met her father, who was completing a master's degree at the University of Taiwan. Both of them left Korea after they married: "My mom was just not feeling good in Korea since it was not conducive to a woman's career," Kimm says. Her father, Young Ho Kimm—who Anglicized his name to Andrew Y. Kimm—worked as a machinist but also started a newspaper, *Kaju Shinmoon*, for his fellow immigrants. He found that

Koreans in L.A. in the beginning were more concerned about news back in Korea than about the local community, his daughter recalls. "I know that both my parents constantly said they could never live in Korea again because the community there was too nosey and homogeneous," she says. "Also the fact that my mom married a younger man and that would have been taboo back in the day."

Esther Kimm earned a BA degree at UCLA in 1991 and became a personnel recruiter for accounting firms and then for aerospace and technology companies, such as Northrop Grumman, SpaceX, and others. In recent years she recruited for Faraday Future, which had more than seven hundred employees and was building an electric car factory in North Las Vegas, Nevada, until problems with financial backing from Leshi Internet and Technology Co. in China ran into money troubles. The factory project was canceled, and uncertainty prevailed about Faraday as Star Kimm left the company in September 2017.

Kimm's father died in 1998. And she takes care of her mother, the former Kum Nyum, who Anglicized her name to Rachel N. Kimm. "The Korean community is cool in one special way," Esther Kimm says. "They provide centers that cater to aging Koreans. My mom gets picked up at 9 a.m. and is driven to her social club, where she can play games earning her points toward gaining a prize. We haven't run out of soy milk since she's attended the senior citizen center."

She has interesting observations about today's attitudes among her fellow Korean Americans. For one thing, they have renewed interest in Korea and current events involving government changes in Seoul and the possibilities of reuniting with North Korea.

"Naturally my eyes will pause on any news from Korea, especially with the impeachment issues of late," she said in 2017. "I am not optimistic about the reunification, however, because there are a lot of unknown forces out there that want to keep Korea split. And although we are one people, the North has "brainwashed" their people and ruled by fear, so it is like a dysfunctional family trying to repair itself. I'm not saying it cannot be mended, but it would take a long time to undo what's been done for many decades."

Kimm has ambitions for her son Joshua, nine, who attends school in Los Angeles and offers critical comments about her Asian work ethic compared to that of more comfortable Americans.

"I don't know about others, but as for me, I raise my son to appreciate our Korean culture and community and to know the differences in approach as we live in the U.S.," she says, recalling her work at Faraday.

The American workers are having to learn how to work with their Chinese counterparts who have never worked in the U.S. prior to Faraday Future. They have to figure out how to communicate, and the Chinese are learning how "thin skinned" we Americans are and that the direct approach doesn't bode well. The "saving face" Asian aspect of business is something we Americans are poor at in practice. Also, the Chinese partners have a work ethic that the Americans just can't follow. They will work until they drop and Americans will go home at 5 p.m., which is unheard of when "there is so much to do," according to the Chinese.

Kimm goes on:

So yes, I think the hardworking ethic that Asians bring to the table is definitely challenging the U.S. workers. It definitely makes me work harder when they are here. I find it interesting that the Chinese workers won't leave before their boss leaves or tells them they can leave. This is true in Korea as well. But Americans are a bit "entitled" or perhaps a little too savvy and care more about quality of life than quantity. For example, when the Chinese investor [JiaYueting and his Leshi Technology Co. associates] came to our offices, and the clock struck 5:30 p.m., our VP and the director had left to go home after a hard day's work. I don't know why, perhaps booouce I was brought up by my very Korean and militant father, I stayed and continued to work. I later found that this little shift in behavior was applauded by them as they saw my butt in my seat while everyone else was gone.

"I guess the Chinese work ethic rubbed off on us," she adds about that experience. "Not that we don't work hard, but we are more cognizant of appearances now that we interface more often with the China office."

Another instructive story is that of Jerry Kang, who is professor of law at UCLA and vice chancellor for Equity, Diversity and Inclusion.[6] He was born in Seoul in 1968 and came with his parents to Los Angeles. He wanted to be a scientist and earned a degree in physics magna cum laude from Harvard University in 1990. But he said in an interview for the Council of Korean Americans, "I was interested in physics because I wanted to be a scientist. But at college, as an immigrant, I wanted to know politically how this American society works so I could do something for people I cared about. And I thought theoretical physics would not be the way to do that. So I studied the law and found that was a way I could work to change things."

Kang took a Juris Doctor degree from Harvard in 1993, clerked for a judge in the court of appeals, and joined the UCLA faculty in 1995. In his career he has become an expert on Asian American affairs and has written about hate crimes, affirmative action, and the Japanese American Internment and its lessons for the War on Terror of the post-2001 decades. On that point, Kang is a coauthor of *Race, Rights and Reparations: The Law and the Japanese American Internment*. In a concluding passage, Kang's point was asking how much we as citizens should defer to the government's claim of a "plausible yet possibly unfounded 'claim of urgent need'" to justify forcing Japanese Americans into internment camps during World War II. We did not, after all, inter German Americans and Italian Americans.[7]

So here is a man born in 1968 into a society that did not then have a policy of supporting fundamental liberties—that in fact had bitter memories of colonialism's injustices—warning clearly about the connection between society's fears and the temptation to persecute its own people. Kang has been honored many times for his teaching and writing on law and justice.

Young Woo is a real estate developer and architect who spoke to the 2013 NetKAL Summit meeting in Los Angeles and more recently in an interview for this book.[8] His firm, Young Woo & Associates, is developing a $350 million Super Pier project in New York, where container-sized store-spaces will become offices for Google and restaurants in a structure that extends into the Hudson River at Fifteenth Street in Manhattan. Now sixty-four, Woo emigrated from Korea to Argentina with his father in 1965 when he was twelve. "My father wanted to go to the United States but it was difficult at that time, so we went to South America instead," Woo says. But in 1972 opportunity opened, and the family came to New York. After a series of jobs, working as a butcher, driving a taxi, Woo enrolled in Pratt Institute and studied architecture. But when he graduated he chose to go into the tough business of real estate development rather than the more artistic architecture.

"I'm one of the only Korean developers in New York," Woo says, and notes that "in Korea, although it is slowly changing, it is difficult in a five-thousand-year-old, tiny country to assemble land for development. Many developers have bad names as people think you're trying to swindle them out of their property." Also, it is very different in Asia. Samsung and Hyundai and other big companies control the market, Woo says. But in New York "developers are respected. Traditional developers are mostly Jewish family firms, intriguing minds and business sense. I learned a lot from them," he says. "Jewish people are like Asian people. They helped me."

Young Woo & Associates has become very successful, buying and remaking buildings in original ways, such as a sky garage, where condo owners can take cars up to their apartment doors. How did Woo learn how to do well in a tough business? His response sounds semi-biblical: "You look for seven good years when you invest and then you pause. Money is always in short supply, but there is always money, if the project is good," Woo says. In 2007, he thought things looked "too good." So he pulled money out and went to Argentina and invested in land for housing and vineyards. But he came back in 2009 and bought a building in the Wall Street area for $107 a square foot—"the price of the plumbing fixtures," he remarks. Within a couple of years, the value had risen to $1,000 per square foot and continued rising.

The Young Woo firm has pioneered "telecom hotels," which creatively repurposed buildings to maximize rent by servicing higher-paying data center tenants. To further attract these tenants, Young Woo activated the otherwise dormant lobbies of these telecom hotels by implementing creative lobby designs and by leasing to appealing retail tenants. "Young people don't want large organizations," he says. Woo and his business partner for thirty years, attorney Margarette (CQ) Lee, also a Korean immigrant, have become leaders in New York's large Korean community.

Margarette Lee has an almost family relationship to Korean Air's Wilshire Grand Center.[9] From the age of nine, Lee traveled to Vietnam with her father Eun Hyun Lee, who was an executive with Hanjin, the shipping company that supplied U.S. and Korean troops during the Vietnam War.

Lee came to the United States with her father in the 1970s, and lived in San Francisco, Hawaii, Chicago, and Seattle and then New York. She studied fine art at Western Washington University and came to New York to get her master's in fine arts and met her husband, Ik-Joong Kang, who is now one of the major Korean artists in the world (with a collection at Los Angeles Museum of Contemporary Art and the Whitney). "But in the beginning it was hard financially to have two artists in the family," Lee says, "so I studied at night and took a law degree from Brooklyn Law School." She is proud to be one of the few women developers—"I'm asked 'whose secretary are you?'" she laughs. Lee has been with Young Woo since 1985.

"Korean community people are doing amazing things," Lee says, reflecting on her friends and younger generations of Korean Americans.

She cites Kyung Yoon, who heads the Korean American Community Foundation. "They raise millions of dollars at their annual galas," Lee says. "Older Koreans in the beginning were not used to such giving. But young generations are used to tax incentives and they say, 'if you do well why not share? It's only good for the community and for your own children at the end of the day.'"

Young Woo and Margarette Lee have enhanced the image of and increased the visibility of Korean Americans, accomplishments that have allowed and will continue to allow Korean Americans to be major forces not just in real estate but in all areas of the American economy.

Kyung Yoon was a television correspondent for Fox News in New York and then a creator and host of documentaries at the World Bank before deciding in 2002 to cofound the Korean American Community Foundation, which gives grants and promotes ways to help low-income Korean families get better jobs and cope with problems.[10] An aim of the foundation also is to encourage Koreans to "reach out to others in the broader community and to give money to good causes." The foundation has now given more than $5 million in grants to community-based organizations. And it has inspired the formation in San Francisco of KACF-SF, a branch of the Korean American Community Foundation that aims to tackle problems among the 22 percent of Bay Area Korean Americans who have low incomes and are without health insurance.

Kwangsoo Kim is a lawyer with offices in Queens, in New York City, and Fort Lee, in northern New Jersey, two areas of large Korean immigrant neighborhoods. Many second-generation Korean Americans have moved on to more suburban neighborhoods, but some of their teenage children are prone to get in trouble just like all other youngsters. So lawyer Kim and others formed the Korean American Youth Foundation to bring help and guidance to the delinquent youngsters and their families. "These are our young people," says lawyer Kim, "and we have to help them stay out of trouble with drugs and drink, delinquency, and stay in school and lead good lives." Kim is talking American urban history. In other times in New York neighborhoods, there was the Police Athletic League, with indoor basketball and boxing rings to "keep kids off the streets." As it was then, so it is now. Generations of Korean Americans are adapting an urban tradition.

In Philadelphia, Raymond John graduated from the University of Pennsylvania premed in 2008 with a BA in psychology and went to New York to pursue further research. But through work at a charity for the homeless in New York, he developed the idea of helping inner-city

Comfort Woman statue, Glendale, CA, commemorating Korean women forced into sex slavery by Japan's military in WW II. Courtesy of Comfort Woman Justice Coalition.

youngsters to pursue education beyond elementary and high school levels, to go to college and improve their careers and their lives. So he founded a nonprofit company named 12-Plus and devised new systems of instruction and encouragement to inspire underserved communities. He returned to Philadelphia and has built up 12-Plus through a belief that education is the key to breaking the cycle of poverty and enabling people to rise in society and live better lives. That happens to be a profound belief among Koreans, because historically their people were denied the chance of education. The company and Raymond John have been honored by the city of Philadelphia.

To sum up, Korean Americans have advanced to the point that they are confident in their achievements to date and ready to take the next steps. This was very clear in the first summit meeting and gala of the Council of Korean Americans in Washington, DC, on October 23–24, 2015.[11] In two days, prominent Korean Americans from all parts of the country were given briefings by government staffers in the White House and the U.S. Congress. John Lim, CKA's early leader, opened the awards banquet saying, "we Korean Americans are privileged to live in the most democratic society in the world. But often we have not participated or made ourselves heard in that democracy. For too long, we have been on the sidelines—some would say 'pushed' to the sidelines. For too long we have not had a seat at the table. We promise tonight we are going to change that."

Lim introduced the keynote speaker Jim Yong Kim, who is just ending a five-year term as president of the World Bank. Kim was born in South Korea, raised in Iowa, and trained as a medical doctor at Harvard University; he founded a doctors' organization that fights disease in Haiti and other poor countries, headed the World Health Organization, and served as president of Dartmouth College before assuming his World Bank post in 2012.

"We Korean Americans have the ability to make an outsized impact on how this country evolves," Kim told the glittering dinner audience. "And also on how this country sees itself as a multicultural society. As hybrids, we Korean Americans have the opportunity to make a huge impact in moving this country forward."

Note the forceful words from a man who has succeeded notably in American life. Jim Kim is not boasting nor is he preaching in speaking of America "evolving" or being a "multicultural society." He is committing himself and Korean Americans to the U.S. of A., their country. It is a commitment that offspring of immigrants have always made, to create a better life for their children and generations to come. Korean Americans exemplify—indeed they proclaim—the promise and fulfillment of immigration to the United States.

Within a year of that first summit meeting, the Council of Korean Americans held another in Washington and emphasized its expanding reach across the nation and the world by including Korean Americans who hold executive positions with Samsung in Seoul, Walt Disney Co. in China, and Morgan Stanley in Hong Kong. And cka began speaking out on critical issues concerning South and North Korea,[12] calling in 2016 for a new approach to North Korea that would emphasize negotiation and peaceful reform of the troubled truce that has lasted sixty-four years since Korean War fighting ended in 1953.

Then in January 2017, the cka issued a statement condemning the Trump Administration's executive order barring immigration from some Muslim countries. The cka is organizing legal services for Korean residents who are in the United States on work permit visas or with green cards that qualify for permanent residence if they renew the permit annually. At its third summit in Washington in October 2017,[13]

CKA members pledged in particular to involve themselves in government at local, state, and federal levels. "Mayors, senators, presidents," as one ambitious speaker put it.

On North Korea, the meeting heard from a journalist who reported for years from Pyongyang, a doctor from Harvard Medical School who led health improvement programs in North Korea, and an official of a private university operating there. Also, CKA members heard talks on immigration, including families covered by the deferred action for childhood arrivals (DACA) program. And the meeting honored Rhea Suh, president of the Natural Resources Defense Council, a three-million strong organization, who spoke on the responsibility of immigrants' children and grandchildren to adapt and work for their new country even as they reflected on the culture of the old.

Similarly, NetKAL, the network of Korean American leaders, has expanded by creating new memberships in Korea itself and by looking ahead to memberships among Koreans in China. "Many Koreans live and work in China," said NetKAL founder and director Je Hoon Lee.

Well beyond their own organizations, Koreans and Korean Americans are earning notice in U.S. business media, including *Forbes* magazine, which publishes lists of successful entrepreneurs.[14] It has hailed Gideon Yu, who has been a venture capital investor in Silicon Valley and chief financial officer of Facebook and Yahoo. He founded Eva Automation, a company in audio and visual technology, and is co-owner of the San Francisco 49ers pro football team. Yu immigrated to Nashville, Tennessee, as a teenager, then studied engineering at Harvard and Stanford and finance at Harvard Business School.

The magazine also has profiled Il Yeon Kwon, who immigrated to New York in 1982 and opened a grocery store in Queens called Han Ah Reum (One Arm Full of Groceries). The store succeeded in New York and New Jersey as H Mart and then expanded to more than fifty H Mart superstores across the United States featuring Korean and Asian foods of all kinds.

Again, those entrepreneurs are profiled because they drive home a point made throughout this book—that immigrants, Koreans, and all other peoples who come to America bring new energy and accomplishment. As John Suh puts it in chapter 5: "It is still true that if you are born outside the United States, you are a hundred times more likely to start a business." Many reasons explain that. First, newcomers are not easily going to climb the ranks of large organizations. Second, in the case of Koreans, they were for half a century a colony of Japan and so not able to find much success in the Japanese corporate system. Beyond Japanese colonization, Koreans historically were born into a society dominated by an aristocracy. You cannot join an aristocracy; you must be born into it. But in this new society of America, your fate does not depend on who your parents or forebears are, but who you are.

So the drive of entrepreneurs stems from instincts that make people immigrants in the first place. They are leaving one society and coming to a new place where they are free to think anew and act anew. You can create your own livelihood, succeed or fail on your own ideas and beliefs—and if you fail, you can get up and try again. America has always held that promise and Americans of all backgrounds have reached for opportunities. They are doing so today—and Koreans and Korean Americans are notable for their energy in renewing the entrepreneurial faith, in striving for accomplishment, and making efforts to help their fellows. Korean Americans, as Jim Yong Kim says, are "making an impact in moving America forward." They are showing America that we are in the Pacific World now and will remain there always. They herald a new understanding, a new horizon.

Yes, as John Lim puts it, Korean Americans have come far in an open and democratic society that welcomed and benefited from their initiatives and hard work. But what should equally be noted is that Korean American success has come against the fortunate backdrop of South Korea's own economic growth in the open trading system of the United States and other developed nations. Korea has benefited also from technology contributions from Japanese industry. From dire poverty, South Korea has risen over the last six decades to become a prosperous and advanced economy.

The total of goods and services produced in 2017 by the South Korean economy—what is called the gross national product, or GNP— was $1.81 trillion, slightly lower than Canada's GNP and a bit more than Russia's and Australia's.[15] South Korea's 50 million people now average a statistical annual income of $36,370, a level that brings it close to such industrialized countries as Italy, which has some 59 million people. For another comparison, the six-county economy of Los Angeles and all of Southern California, with 22 million people, produces $1.3 trillion of goods and services annually and has a GNP per capita of $56,000.

Moreover, the world's most advanced nation technologically is argu- ably South Korea. It is the "wired" nation, with more of its people using the Internet at faster speeds than anywhere else. For example, people in Korea can download a movie to their phone or tablet in twenty-two seconds, compared to roughly an hour for folks in the United States. And now the race is on to upgrade to wireless services at five gigabytes of bandwidth—a thousand times faster than present limits. That will bring on devices through which one can electronically run a factory, a health clinic, or a home. The race for 5G is worldwide, with companies in the United States, Europe, and the rest of Asia intensifying research and development.

Korea and the United States are the closest of trade partners. In 2012, both nations signed the U.S.–Korea Trade Agreement, which eliminates tariffs and spurs commerce between the two. Trade agreements across the oceans or across our borders became political flashpoints in presidential elections of 2016. And to be sure, the U.S.–Korea Trade Agreement could be endangered by antitrade thinking and policies of the current White House. So it is useful to demonstrate anew that trade is a two-way street, now as ever. A few stories of giant Korean *chaebol* companies and their interactions with U.S. business can illustrate that point.

Pohang Iron and Steel Co., or POSCO, is one example.[16] Pohang Steel began in 1973 because President Chung Hee Park wanted South Korea to have a car industry, and before you can build a car, you need a steel industry. So POSCO was started with war reparation funds that the U.S. government made Japan pay to the new country of South Korea after World War II. The company poured its first one million tons of steel in 1973 into a new plant built with the most modern equipment and technology—just like all the other steel plants built in war-torn Europe and Asia after the war. Meanwhile, American steel plants for the most part did not greatly modernize but just kept going with the blast furnaces and equipment that had helped to win the war. That became pertinent in 1986, when U.S. Steel Corp. suffered financial losses at its plant in Pittsburg, California. The company had to modernize then and so it entered a fifty-fifty joint venture with Pohang called USS-POSCO Industries, or UPI.

Together the venture partners invested $450 million to bring in new steel equipment from Germany and Japan along with modern computer technology from America's General Electric Corp. and Honeywell International Inc. Employees of UPI were sent to Korea, Japan, and Germany to learn the new steel technologies. And a revitalized steel mill opened in April 1989 with speeches from U.S. Steel and Pohang Steel executives. In an article in the *Los Angeles Times*, U.S. Steel's president, Thomas Graham, explained the new globalization of industry. "In steel the state of the art is advanced by building a new plant and we didn't have the money to build a new plant," Graham said, though he added that the newest computer technology was all American. With the new mill, the UPI venture and Pittsburg prospered and prospers still thanks to additional investment made over decades since then.

Pohang Steel figured in another hands-across-the-sea story in 2002. Modern China, formerly "Red China," had expanded its steel production to such an extent that Korea's steelmaking was under pressure from low-priced competition. So Pohang looked to invest in newer industries. It set up a biotechnology task force in San Diego and announced that it would invest $400 million over five years in fledgling biotech companies in California. It appointed a Korean American oil executive, Leonard Kim, who had retired from Royal Dutch Shell to head the biotech venture. Well, biotechnology has marched on, and most new medicines in recent decades have arisen from the biosciences. Pohang Steel and Korea's own research efforts in medicine and healthcare have benefited from those forward-looking investments.

Another kind of story is Hyundai Motor America, which has built a new headquarters in Fountain Valley, California, and advanced to an 8 percent share of the U.S. car market with sales of more than 760,000 automobiles a year.[17] The auto company Hyundai, a Korean word that means *modern*, is one division of a large engineering and construction company started in the 1950s by Chung Ju-yung, who built bases for the U.S. Eighth Army and went on to build all over the world. He sent workers to Saudi Arabia in the 1970s when oil money fueled a boom in that country. Hyundai also made early cars for South Korean customers with help from Japan's Mitsubishi Motors.

Success in Korea's market emboldened Hyundai to come to the United States in 1986, when Japan's car companies were holding down their imports due to pressure from the U.S. Congress. Toyota and Datsun were also raising prices at that time. "So Hyundai saw opportunity and came in with a $6,000 car," said Finbarr O'Neill, an American lawyer who had joined Hyundai Motor America as general counsel. The car named Excel was an instant success, and sales shot up in 1986 and 1987. But the car had problems of quality, and those became apparent to customers as early as 1988; sales began to decline—and kept on declining right into the decade of the 1990s. Indeed, Hyundai cars became the butt of jokes on late-night TV.

"The company was looking over the precipice of oblivion in the U.S.," says O'Neill, who became chief operating officer and then president and chief executive of Hyundai's U.S. company in 1998. But Hyundai did not go into oblivion. It became a legend in the auto business because it improved and dared. Back home in Korea, according to *The New Korea*, a 2010 book on Korean business by Myung Oak Kim and Sam Jaffe, management caught on to the quality problems and began to make better cars. O'Neill meanwhile visited his dealers all over the country and was told that the Hyundais were now much better than their poor reputation. So Hyundai Motor America made a daring move: It introduced a 100,000-mile ten-year warranty with every vehicle. That set the auto world buzzing, and customers came back reckoning they didn't risk horrendous repair bills. Hyundai's business improved, and so did that of its 33-percent-owned affiliate, Kia Motors, which has a design and technical center in Irvine.

O'Neill, who left Hyundai in 2003 to head Mitsubishi Motors and now is president of the automotive research firm J.D. Power & Associates, sees Hyundai's comeback as a case of adaptation to the new world. Executives who came over from Korea learned that they must treat U.S. auto dealers as independent businesspeople and partners rather than employees to be ordered around.

It adapted in other ways, O'Neill explains. When a Hyundai dealer in the Boston area started a fund for handicapped children called the Jimmy Fund, Hyundai management soon applied Jimmy Fund charities to all its district operations in the United States. Philanthropy has continued. Recently Hyundai completed a multiyear $10 million donation to Children's Hospital of Orange County. And in 2015, Hyundai pledged a ten-year program of support for the Los Angeles County Museum of Art. The carmaker's funds will support exhibits of Korean art for the museum.

In a different cultural adaptation, Hyundai last year became a leading sponsor of the National Football League, and Kia Motors is the "automotive partner" of the National Basketball Association. It doesn't get more "mainstream" than that.

Finally, Samsung Electronics, the largest conglomerate of all, tells many meaningful stories.[18] Samsung was founded in 1938 as a rice trader when Korea was a colony of Japan. Lee Byung-choll founded the company with a vision of exporting dried seaweed and pickled fish to China. It operated through World War II but then collapsed, only to be rebuilt after the war as a leading food trader. Then immediately after the Korean War, Samsung built a textile mill and grew as a clothing manufacturer, making a name for Korean-made garments in other countries. Founder Lee then expanded the firm into life insurance and shipbuilding. In 1969 Samsung Electronics was formed to manufacture home appliances, including washing machines, microwave ovens, and television sets.

Along with making TV sets, Lee Byung-choll purchased a struggling semiconductor company, reasoning correctly that electronic chips would become part of every appliance, including computers and products barely envisioned in the 1970s and early 1980s. Samsung grew with the home appliance business, both at home and for export. Its prominence took a leap in 1988 when Samsung emerged as the chief commercial sponsor of the Olympic Games in Seoul.

By that time, Lee Byung-choll had died and his son, Lee Kun-hee, had taken over the top job with ambitions to make Samsung a world-leading company. At a 1993 meeting of Samsung's top executives in Frankfurt, Germany, Lee delivered an order that rang through Samsung corporate offices. "Change everything except your wife and children," he said. A quarter century later, Samsung has grown to be a world-leading corporation in many fields, with $200 billion in annual revenues—$60 billion of that in the United States. Its U.S. headquarters are in Ridgefield, New Jersey, and centers for Samsung Electronics are in San Jose and other Silicon Valley cities, plus manufacturing centers in Austin, Texas. But Samsung and Korea's connections to the United States are not a simple story. Samsung developed as a leading maker of smartphones, the chief rival of Apple Computer, because the company and South Korea took up the operating system developed by Qualcomm Inc. of San Diego.[19]

Briefly, the story goes back to the late 1980s, as Qualcomm was developing a wireless operating system for mobile phones called code division multiple access (CDMA), which allowed cell phone calls to be sent over multiple frequencies, thereby maximizing available bandwidth. It could do this because CDMA broke down calls into packets of information, sent them out, and then rebuilt them at the recipient's phone, just the way the Internet operates. Qualcomm, founded in 1985 by Irwin Jacobs and Dr. Andrew Viterbi, was developing the new system under a project of the U.S. Defense Advanced Research Projects Agency.

Code division multiple access was superior to a system used in the early days of cellular telephony called Global System Mobile, or GSM, which was favored by European phone manufacturers. So the Europeans then tried to have the Qualcomm system disqualified by international telecom standards. But the superiority of CDMA won it a place in Asia, starting with South Korea. That was in the 1980s, and Qualcomm's

CDMA went on to become the indispensable technological core of the worldwide wireless phone industry.

Qualcomm and Samsung remain technological partners today. Currently they are collaborating on the most advanced processor for cellular phones. Qualcomm has developed the system and is having Samsung manufacture the high-tech chips in a long-term agreement that began in 2005. Also, both the American and Korean companies are pursuing five-gigabyte technology to expand the capabilities of telecommunications technology. Thus they provide a decades-long demonstration that global technology and trade are two-way streets, not one-way or dead-end alleys.

In the closing days of 2017, Samsung was enjoying great success with a new series of smartphones, while Qualcomm was dealing with an enormous $130 billion takeover offer from Broadcom, a pioneering U.S. semiconductor company now headquartered in Singapore that was moving its corporate headquarters to Delaware. But the U.S. government stopped Broadcom's takeover attempt, ruling it a threat to the United States' national security. The ruling's effect is to defend U.S. leadership in a time of competition from China's technologically advancing companies.

Qualcomm will continue its 5G research and so will Samsung as both companies, collaborating in some areas, competing in others, continue to strive for telecom technology leadership.

Meanwhile Samsung has built itself into Korea's leading conglomerate, or *chaebol*, and become a leading force for Korean cultural outreach. In 1993 Samsung spun off part of its early food businesses into CJ, or CheilJedang, which means "First Sugar." The company also is engaged in biotechnology and pharmaceutical production as well as entertainment. Companies of CJ, such as CJ America Entertainment and Marketing, are responsible for spreading Korean television dramas to China, Indonesia, Iran, and many other countries. K-Pop musical groups entertain young people worldwide.

Samsung Galaxy smartphones led even Apple iPhones in worldwide sales until 2016–2017, when Galaxy Note 7 models began to explode. Samsung withdrew that model from world markets, losing more than $5 billion and suffering great damage to its reputation. However, current Galaxy models are helping Samsung recover its stature. In response to Trump Administration trade policies, Samsung has announced that it will locate a new smartphone manufacturing plant in the United States.

The company also has been involved in Korea's political scandals.

Lee Jay Yong, named as new managing director of the giant company and grandson of Samsung founder Lee Byung-choll, has been arrested and charged with giving bribes to an associate of Korea's now-impeached president. The charges against big corporate leaders and the impeachment itself were part of a general revolt by Koreans against the government-business system that has, in effect, ruled South Korea for decades, reported Peter Pae, bureau chief of *Bloomberg News* in Seoul, and fellow reporters.[20] (Pae himself is a Korean American who came to Los Angeles at age six in 1972 with his father, Richard Hamtok Pae, who started the first Korean-language television station in L.A. Richard Pae also worked with the Korean Democracy movement along with Kim Dae Jung, who became Korea's president from 1998 to 2003. Peter Pae graduated from UCLA and reported for the *Wall Street Journal* and *Washington Post* before writing and editing for the *Los Angeles Times* for fifteen years, then moving to Seoul in 2015 for *Bloomberg News*.)

Yet historic changes arose in Korea beginning in 2017, as the United States and China got more involved and South Korea elected a new president, Moon Jae-in. Even as North Korea loudly threatened to launch nuclear weapons at everyone in sight, President Trump, China's President Xi Jinping, and Moon Jae-in conferred in meetings and at conferences of Asian nations.

Then in 2018 South Korea hosted the Winter Olympic Games and invited North Korea to send athletes and officials to participate. It proved a breakthrough in many ways. North Korea's leader, Chairman Kim Jong Un, and South Korea's President Moon scheduled meetings late in April, and President Trump scheduled a meeting with Kim in early June. This year could prove to be truly historic. And Korean Americans are sure to be affected directly and indirectly by the old homeland of Korea by its development as a hoped-for unified country and its relations with the United States and China.

Chapter 7 will look to the future of the Korean American community in politics, business, entertainment, international relations, and the philosophy and vision of an always-changing multicultural America.

Historic Challenges, Beacons for the Future

As Korean Americans commemorated the twenty-fifth anniversary of the 1992 Los Angeles Riots and celebrated the completion of the Wilshire Grand Center in 2017, the Korean community faced new challenges and supported new causes and ambitious goals.

Theirs is no longer just a familiar tale of immigrants in America from a very poor Republic of Korea but a developing story of American people—with ties of family, business, and culture to a now-prospering old homeland—trying to influence politics, philosophy, and vision in their new country.

The promise of America is there for them as always, but new challenges arise from wrenching change in Korea and from a new administration in Washington that threatens to shut out Korean and other foreign students and to deny work to those students who are completing their studies here. "Students and universities are discouraged in doing any kind of exchange program with the U.S.," reports Douglas Lee, founder of Stanley Prep, a Seoul-based company that trains Korean students for study and work overseas.[1]

"If America is seen as less welcoming, that is a cause for concern," says Sam Yoon, executive director of the Council for Korean Americans in Washington.[2]

Bear in mind a huge share of immigration is family-based; family members sponsoring other family members. That could change in a new immigration policy regime. But this new policy is relevant to lots of undocumented Koreans—some estimates say as many as 180,000 Koreans are living in the U.S. illegally. Many of them are "dreamers" or undocumented children—Koreans are among the highest share of Asians who don't have legal status. They're the ones who are really worried now about deportation.

The change came like a thunderclap to what had been growing co-operation in every aspect of education, medicine, and business between Korean Americans and their counterparts in Korea. Thus a shadow hovers over the community even as it has attained so much in its new land. This chapter will tell of Korean American progress made in technology and media, politics, and local government and even in U.S. international policy. The Korean community is bringing vigor and vision to the American Way of Life. That's why I've referred to it as a "beacon for our future."

On a trip to Seoul in November 2016,[3] I witnessed the confidence of Korean young people as more than 2,000 gathered at an entrepreneurial conference to hear Eugene Wei of Facebook Inc. from Silicon Valley talk of the Oculus Rift headset and the future of virtual reality in their realms of entertainment and information technology. They looked forward eagerly to working collaboratively while traveling back and forth between Korea and the United States.

At another gathering, the Seoul Summit meeting of the Network of Korean American Leaders,[4] Soh Yeong Roh spoke of her work in artificial intelligence. As director of the Art Center Nabi in Seoul, she has developed robot models that hold conversations with people and even display emotion. She is a recognized expert in robot interaction with humans. A graduate of the College of William & Mary in Virginia, she has studied at the University of Chicago and has a master's in education from Stanford. She is a daughter of Roh Tae-woo, former president of South Korea, and her own daughter is an officer in the Republic of Korea Navy.

More to the point, Roh has worked with IBM on its Watson system and with Google and Microsoft. At the NetKAL meeting in Seoul, she showed videos of robots exhibiting emotions and interacting with herself and others. She told the audience that she would probably move back to Silicon Valley to continue her research work. Thus Soh Yeong Roh is a prime example of Korea–U.S. collaboration and accomplishment.

And there will be more examples to come. Suok Noh, a veteran of twenty-five years as a managing director of Goldman Sachs, is president of NetKAL's advisory board.[5] He is also a venture partner of Redbadge Pacific Capital, which invests in technology startup companies across Asia. He spoke at the Seoul conference of opportunities in the growing fields of global entertainment and technology and of plans for NetKAL to hold future summit meetings in China. The message underlines the remarkable expanse of Korean drama and show business events that inform and entertain millions around the world.

Of course, the world today is well acquainted with Korean culture thanks to K-Pop music, the Gangnam style that attracts the young of all nationalities, and by Korean dramas in translation and Korean programs on streaming video services to mobile phones and tablets. It is a boom industry called Hallyu, or Korean Wave, a term coined by the Chinese to describe the worldwide spread of Korean entertainment, including games, films, and pop videos. "It used to be that Korean was *uncool* but now to be Korean is *cool,*" says Angela Killoren, chief operating officer of cj America, Entertainment & Media, a Los Angeles-based arm of a Seoul-based conglomerate that produces food, pharmaceuticals, biotechnology compounds, and research and entertainment.[6]

Killoren's company annually produces kcon (literal meaning, "Korean wave convention events"), which are combination pop concerts, food, and fashion fairs. In 2015, a kcon drew fifty-eight thousand young people, non-Korean and Korean alike, in three days at the L.A. Convention Center and another drew 17,000 in a one-day kcon event in the New York area. In 2017, kcon drew 128,000 in Los Angeles and New York concerts—following successful concerts in Mexico City, Abu Dhabi, Australia, Paris, and Tokyo in a two-year period. "We continue to grow the kcons because it's an outreach to young Korean Americans and non-Koreans to access the culture," Killoren says. "For young people to be able to have pride in their culture is one of the reasons I do this," she adds.

Killoren is a daughter of a Korean mother and an American father, Kenneth Killoren, a native of Wisconsin, who was the first president of Sogang University, which opened in Seoul in 1960. Angela Killoren was born in Chicago but grew up in Seoul from age three, once her parents had returned to Korea to work and live. Her mother, Joanne Lee, one of the first bilingual professionals at that time, handled international conferences and visits from President Gerald Ford, Henry Kissinger, and boxer Muhammad Ali. Angela later graduated from New York's Columbia University, where she earned a degree in East Asian Languages and Cultures.

"I was blessed to have a very strong bicultural and bilingual background—where I learned to appreciate the assets of each of U.S. and Korean cultures," Killoren says today. "Pride in my culture is a strong motivator, but it is not one-directional for bringing Korea to the U.S. I think our larger mandate is to create a multicultural community wherein contemporary Korean culture has a place in the U.S. and that Koreans also embrace the incredibly diverse global fandom as part of their own, not just bask in the validation."

In the work she does with CJ America, Killoren notes with pride that in international entertainment, Korean films and videos rank very high—third in the world behind only English- and Spanish-language features. Indeed, Korean programming in translation captivates TV markets in Iran and the Middle East and many markets in South America, as well as in Indonesia, China, Japan, and all of Asia. The wave started with *Winter Sonata*, a TV drama that first aired in 2002. It became an unprecedented international hit in Japan and China and then throughout the rest of the world. Many more dramas have followed, along with pop stars in singing and dancing groups, such as Girls Generation, CNBLUE, Seventeen, and scores of others. One quality the K-Pop groups have shown the world is the exuberance of young Koreans. The Korean government has backed this spread of culture financially, and Samsung has helped by translating programming across the world.

The dramas have achieved success in the United States also on Korean-language stations and mobile Internet platforms. The technological revolution in recent years has created a new media business that allows videos to be streamed on the Internet and watched—even "binge"-watched—by young people on computers, mobile phones, and tablets. A good example is DramaFever Corp., which was founded in 2008 by two Korean Americans, Seung Bak and Suk Park, who had a vision of bringing international quality television to young audiences. "Our core audience is young women, the female millennials eighteen to thirty-four who watch streaming videos on phones or tablets," says Bak.[7] "The videos might be produced in Korea or Japan, but the fundamental values are shared across the world. You can see other countries and cultures through entertainment."

Bak and Park, who both went to the University of Rochester, started their company by putting up $50,000 to buy rights to distribute videos over a Korean-language station in New York. They kept their day jobs—Park as a managing director of Ziff Davis, publishers of print and online products, and Bak as communications director for investment-banking firms. As their new business grew to tens of thousands of monthly users, they raised venture capital, expanded staff, and kept on growing. DramaFever is now the largest video-on-demand site of Asian televised content, with twenty million users monthly.

Audiences for their dramas are a great mix of white, Latino, black, and Asian—with the majority non-Asian. The appeal of their films, said a Philadelphia mother of three, is a "definite lack of explicit sex. The writers are forced to tell a story. American TV has got to be too much with sex and violence and language. People want solid values and morals."

The business became a financial success. In 2014 Japan's Softbank Media Group bought DramaFever for $100 million. Then in 2016, Warner Bros. bought it from Softbank for an undisclosed amount. Park and Bak are now diversifying DramaFever's content with telenovelas from South America and videos from Europe. Meanwhile, the company's Korean content recently got a big boost from cj America, which made a multiyear deal with DramaFever to distribute eight K dramas, ten new feature films, and 350 hours of other drama and variety shows. Mark Shaw, chief executive of cj E & M America, said, "as Korean entertainment continues to grow in popularity and influence in the U.S. and around the world, we look forward to growing this partnership together."

The DramaFever story speaks to more than show business success. The financial ability of Korean American entrepreneurs to raise venture capital and build a company that qualifies to be acquired on international markets is a far cry from the pool-your-money *keh* financing of earlier Korean family businesses. "I find it a natural progression," says Stewart Kim, founder and chairman of PGP Capital Advisers investment bank.[8] "As opposed to being an insular group of people, Korean Americans are becoming culturally successful in the broader sense of integrating into high-profile institutions of American society. We need more Koreans to contribute to this society in noneconomic ways, as representatives of public companies and in technology and philanthropy, to become part of the Establishment."

Stewart Kim himself is a pioneer example. He was born in Ohio, where his parents had moved from Korea in 1981 to study at Ohio University and Oberlin College. After earning degrees at Dartmouth and the Wharton School at the University of Pennsylvania, Kim became a managing director of Merrill Lynch in New York. He decided in 2002 to move to Southern California because the Korean community was building up. He started PGP Capital because "Korean businesses needed access to institutional capital markets and major corporate relationships." Kim took on Latino and Chinese entrepreneurs and bankers as advisors and business partners to give his firm broad access to financial communities.

In 2007, he engineered a deal in which golfer Jack Nicklaus's Golden Bear International Inc. formed a partnership with a New York bank and received an investment of $145 million to distribute Nicklaus-brand golf equipment and golf course design services all over Asia. "Jack could

Friendship Bell (Enhanced Photo), San Pedro, donated by Korea at U.S. Bicentennial, 1976. Engravings show Statue of Liberty, U.S., and Goddess of Liberty, Korea. Photo by Patricia Flanigan.

have picked any Wall Street firm, but he chose us," Kim says with understandable pride. In 2005 PGP brought Earthlink into a $440 million joint venture with SK Telecom, Korea's largest wireless phone operator. PGP Capital today advises clients in nine states.

Still, Stewart Kim senses frustration today in the Korean community. "Despite broader achievements and even leadership in business, education, and other sectors, the fields of politics and, yes, even popular entertainment are still viewed as tougher to crack for a host of reasons I won't get into," he says. "So finding other Asian communities that share similar integration and policy goals is a path many have chosen." Kim himself is backing California Treasurer John Chiang, son of immigrants from Taiwan, who has Pan-Asian support in running for governor of the state in the 2018 election.

Other Korean Americans are taking up the call as well. Lawyer John Lim, early chairman of the Council of Korean Americans, says, "we want national office for the influence it can bring. It's not a question of Republican or Democrat," he adds. "You cannot be isolated. The Pan-Asian approach spells a future direction for U.S. politics." In 2017, Lim and CKA's Washington director Sam Yoon urged support for a losing candidate, Robert Lee Ahn, who lost a runoff election for the U.S. Congress. After the loss, Yoon focused on the positive outlook for Pan-Asian political clout. "I see great promise. I am hearing about other Korean Americans in Orange County [California] and in New York, Massachusetts, and Georgia, gearing up to run in 2018. I have been a Korean American political watcher for years, and there is something in the water now. I am sure it is Trump. But increased Korean American activism and engagement over the past few years I believe is emboldening individuals to run."

Yoon in fact was the first Asian American to run for and win elected office in Boston, where he served four years on its city council. Holder of a master's degree in public policy from Harvard, he ran unsuccessfully for mayor of Boston in 2009. He moved to Washington in 2010 as an appointee in the Labor Department under President Obama.

There is both pride and hope in the Korean community for David Min in Irvine, California, and Daniel Koh in Boston, Massachusetts. Min, professor of law at the University of California, Irvine, is running for the U.S. Congress in the 45th district, which includes the cities of Irvine, Anaheim Hills, Rancho Santa Margarita, and Mission Viejo among others.[9] It is traditionally Republican, but things are changing as the district's residents now are one-quarter Asian and Pacific Islander. The Forty-Fifth voted for Hillary Clinton in 2016 over Donald Trump.

Min, forty-one, is a son of Korean immigrants who came to Rhode Island's Brown University in 1972 and settled in San Francisco, where David Min was born in 1976. He is a graduate of the University of Pennsylvania and Harvard Law and worked for nearly two decades as an enforcement attorney at the Securities and Exchange Commission in Washington and as an adviser to Representative Charles Schumer, minority leader of the House. He and his wife, Jane Stoever, moved to Irvine to raise their three children five years ago. Both are on the University of California, Irvine (UCI) faculty.

He was aroused to run for Congress, Min says, after President Trump tried to impose a travel ban on people from seven Muslim countries. "When you think about what brought my parents here, it was the core American values of tolerance, diversity, economic opportunity, and social mobility. What Trump is doing is un-American," Min said on television news. "If we don't stand up for people who are targeted right now, we will be next," he went on. "It's not a partisan issue. Are you going to let something happen that could fundamentally change the character of this country?"

Min ran in a June primary for the Democratic nomination to challenge Rep. Mimi Walters in the November 2018 election, but lost to fellow UCI professor Katie Porter. He will continue to engage in politics, Min says.

Daniel Koh, chief of staff to Mayor Martin Walsh of Boston, is running for the U.S. Congress from the Third Congressional District of Massachusetts.[10] A first-generation Korean American, Koh is the son of two physicians, Dr. Harold Koh, onetime commissioner of public health for Massachusetts, and Dr. Claudia Arrigg. Dan Koh, thirty-two, graduated from Harvard and earned an MBA from Harvard Business School. He has worked in city government as an aide to a previous mayor and in New York for Arianna Huffington as manager of the *Huffington Post*, an online news and opinion site.

Koh was only twenty-nine when he became chief of staff to Boston's current mayor and is moving fast now to try for the U.S. Congress in 2018. Koh will have challengers for the Democratic nomination, so he has begun campaigning throughout his district, which stretches from the Boston suburbs to scores of cities and towns in the western part of the state. Yet he was able to raise more than $800,000 in his first month of campaigning, after resigning from Boston's City Hall. Koh's asset in the money side of politics is a connection to the Korean community nationwide, including fundraising in Los Angeles in December 2017.

That competitive spirit has been building for a few years. The Korean community in Los Angeles celebrated in 2015, when David Ryu won election to the Los Angeles City Council.[11] The election was notable for several reasons. Ryu is the first Korean American elected to the fifteen-member council that governs the city, and he is only the second Asian American elected in the council's 165-year history. Michael Woo, a Chinese American, served on the City Council from 1985 to 1993. (Woo then ran for the office of L.A. mayor and was defeated.)

Significantly, Ryu did not win election in a predominantly Korean or even Asian American district but from constituencies stretching from Sherman Oaks in the San Fernando Valley, over the mountains and eastward to Los Feliz and down to areas near Wilton Place, where Ryu himself grew up. Nor did he run an ethnic-oriented campaign but appealed to voters by raising money door to door in his districts and stressing local reforms such as fixing the streets and responding to constituent appeals. He won a runoff against an aide to a popular councilman who was leaving the post due to term limits.

To be sure, a City Council seat may not sound like much, but with fifteen councilors serving a population of four million in the city of Los Angeles, each council member has 250,000 constituents. And the city is governed largely by its council, as the L.A. mayor has less statutory power than mayors of New York, Chicago, and other big cities. So Ryu's election attests to open opportunity in Los Angeles when a novice immigrant politician, forty-one years old last year (2017), can win a major office in a single bound. "This country is the only place I would have the opportunity to run for office and actually win," Ryu says. "And, yes, Korean Americans are underrepresented. But this is where other underrepresented people will support and vote for you."

Ryu came to the United States with his parents at age six in 1982. His mother was a nurse and his father a teacher, both college graduates who immigrated to L.A. after the 1965 law made it possible. "But it was necessary that they were educated," the councilman says today. "If you were poor, you couldn't come under that 1965 law." Ryu grew up in a typical L.A. neighborhood, mostly Latino with a few Japanese and Vietnamese people. "I watched the *Brady Bunch* but I wasn't white," Ryu remarks. But he became interested in social problems at age seventeen, when after the 1992 Los Angeles Riots, he says, "I went with a Latino and African American because I spoke Korean (on a mission from high school), and I learned about small mom-and-pop liquor stores in South and East L.A. and race disputes and immigration reform."

Indeed, Ryu recalled those high school days at the 2017 Sa I Gu Commemoration, where he encountered Nathan Redfern, who had been Ryu's African American partner visiting riot-torn stores a quarter century earlier. "Stores owners would talk to Redfern because he was with me, and families in the African American community would talk to me because I was with him," said Ryu laughing. Both men lauded the current improved community relationships.

Ryu graduated from UCLA in 1997 and thought of going in the Peace Corps but took a job in the office of L.A. County supervisor Yvonne Brathwaite Burke, who was fighting for recognition of social problems in the black community. So Ryu says he "didn't have to go halfway around the world to help people." He got involved in prison reform, healthcare, housing, and the many issues of urban populations everywhere.

Today he looks ahead to Los Angeles getting the Summer Olympics of 2028 and rings the chimes. "This is a great city with so much vision and potential," he says. "Korean Americans can be the bridge between east and west." Stewart Kim called Ryu's election a "first step" in a talk last year.

Across the country, the Korean community has produced many first steps in recent years. A report put together in 2013 at Queens College in New York fills twenty-eight pages of Korean American elected, administrative, and judicial officials from New York to Los Angeles and states in between, prominently including Washington, DC. In New York, Ron Kim represents a district in Queens in the State Assembly. Closer to home, the current mayor of Irvine is Steven Choi, immigrant from Korea who was once a language instructor with the Peace Corps. And the former mayor of Irvine is Sukhee Kang (see chapter 3), who served in the Korean Army and immigrated to Orange County in 1977.

But 2017 was a testing time for Korean Americans because North Korea once again was launching rockets into the sea and threatening to increase the power of its nuclear weapons.[12] South Korea and the United States were countering with warnings, and President Trump conferred in 2017 with China's president Xi Jinping to make Kim Jong Un, the North Korean dictator, cool down. The United States expressed steadfast support for South Korea and Japan, and Trump sent Vice President Mike Pence to loudly declare that support in Seoul in 2017.

Also change was everywhere in that year. South Korean President Park Geun-hye, was impeached in April 2017, and her successor, Moon Jae-in, was elected president in June. The changes marked new approaches for Korean Americans "who have not been galvanized to any significant degree since the L.A. Riots," said Sam Yoon of CKA. "A lot of activists said their new cause is North Korea."

Yoon speaks about change over generations. "Older folks like my parents are in their seventies; they remember the war from when they were kids and have a view of North Korea that is decidedly more conservative. But the middle-aged and younger generations, whether they are new immigrants or were born in the U.S., will have a more open view."

John Lim of CKA sees opportunity. "Korean Americans are uniquely positioned to influence the U.S. government without the fear of being labeled as the Chin-Buk [friendly with North Korea] faction," Lim says. "But until CKA got formed in 2011, there was never a national organization that could serve as a unified platform from which Korean Americans could make a meaningful impact in the geopolitical landscape. So, we are very hopeful that CKA can step up to the plate in this regard."

North Korea has been a problem for decades for Koreans all over the world. The Communist dictatorship has denied families the right to visit relatives. The Korean community in the United States has long asked for help on the issue of a hundred thousand families separated by the truce at the 38th parallel that ended the Korean War in 1953. There was no peace treaty then or since, and the Korean peninsula remains divided between North and South. In the 1980s and again in 2000 there were brief periods when separated families could visit at the Demilitarized Zone area.

Meanwhile Korean Americans have gotten personally involved in helping refugees from North Korea.[13] Grace Jo spoke to the NetKAL Summit in New York in 2015, telling of her father being tortured and starved to death in North Korea and her mother and sister being tortured. Grace Jo herself, one of 170 North Korean refugees who have settled in the United States, escaped into China twice but was returned to the North Korean state. Finally in 2006, an American missionary pastor, Philip Buck, bribed North Korean agents to let her and a sister escape to China, where the United Nations then enabled them to come to the United States. Jo lives near Washington, DC, and works as a dental assistant while studying to earn a college degree. She helps her sister in running a nonprofit organization, NKinUSA, which helps North Korean refugees.

That work goes on, as does the work of Mike Kim, a financial planner who gave up his business in Chicago in 2003 to travel to the North Korean border of China.[14] His mission was to help North Korean refugees escape that country. He found that young women in North Korea were subject to sex trafficking, so in secret he led a group of such women into China and to the U.S. Embassy in Beijing, where they were safe and could be processed for immigration to the United States. He wrote a book, *Escaping North Korea*, and lectures widely today about refugees and conditions in North Korea.

Joseph Kim, author of *Under the Same Sky: From Starvation in North Korea to Salvation in America*, is now twenty-eight years old.[15] In 2002, at age twelve, he lost his father to starvation and his mother and sister disappeared looking for food. He grew up with relatives in Hoeryong, near the Chinese border. But food was from scarce to unavailable, so at age sixteen he escaped to China, where religious people brought him to Liberty in North Korea, a political organization helping refugees escape the Communist state. He was then able to get to America and go to high school and college. He has become a speaker around the United States and abroad, urging help for the people of North Korea, thanks to connections with Radio Korea International Broadcasting.

Meanwhile, North Korea, under heavy sanctions by the United States, has not prospered in the six decades since the Korean War. At present it is reported by *The Economist* magazine to be trying to reform its agriculture by allowing farmers to profit from their output and its industries by freeing them somewhat from state control. But it is far behind. North Korea, population twenty-five million, has an annual economic output of only $29 billion, roughly equal to the economic output of the state of Vermont, population around 625,000.[16] South Korea, population fifty million people, meanwhile has an annual GDP of some $1.8 trillion, more than that of Russia or Australia, with a GDP per person of $36,370. North Korea, in short, looks like a failing state.

But "it is not going to collapse," says Spencer Kim of the Pacific Century Institute.[17] China will not let it collapse for one thing, he says. "The truth is that China does not want unification of Korea that would put a U.S. ally on its border—nor would it welcome thousands of Korean refugees immigrating into eastern parts of China. And South Korea needs the U.S. fully engaged in Northeast Asia if its security is to be assured," Kim says. His company CBOL Corporation manufactures technical products for the U.S. defense industry and those of other countries. He has long counseled that South Korea and the United States should help North Korea to change by, say, bringing it into international projects, such as an oil pipeline from Russia to both Koreas and Japan. They could help build North Korean energy infrastructure specifically based on nuclear power plants—if nuclear weapons work were closed down.

Clearly, Kim would light one candle rather than curse the darkness, and he has hope for the future of the Korean peninsula. But so do many Korean American leaders, including experts who speak confidentially about military realities on the Korean peninsula. Several of these experts in a joint interview for this book say current talk of long-range missiles and nuclear weapons are a distraction. The real military threat from the North toward the Republic of Korea consists of ten thousand long-range howitzer cannons and rockets that could devastate Seoul in any barrage. That is interesting, of course, but the experts also concede that such an attack would start a new world war in Asia, drawing in China, the United States, Japan, and half the world.

So rather than contemplate the unthinkable, what is to be hoped for realistically? Conceivably there could be negotiations between South and North Korea leading to a peace agreement—perhaps a peace treaty to replace the angry truce that has continued for six-plus decades. Indeed, President Trump and China's President Xi Jinping publicly endorsed peaceful negotiations in 2017. And Korean communities in the United States are now calling for peace in their old homeland. In Fairfax, Virginia, for example, home to 100,000 Koreans and Korean Americans, the community issued a statement hoping for peace talks.

In Los Angeles, members of NetKAL turned out in 2016 to hear former U.S. congressman Charles Rangel of New York call on Korean Americans to help bring peaceful reunification to Korea by petitioning Congress and by joining efforts to help the people of North Korea.[18] (Korea has always been a special cause for Representative Rangel, who was wounded in battle in North Korea in 1952, before coming home with a Bronze Star, gaining an education and a law degree, and serving forty-six years in the U.S. House of Representatives, from which he is now retired.)

Also, in 2016 the chairman of *Joong Ang Ilbo*, one of the largest newspaper and media groups in South Korea, told a Pacific Century Institute audience of a Peace Odyssey trip that thirty-two leading Korean intellectuals took in 2015 across the nine-hundred-mile border region of North Korea and China.[19] The group concluded, Chairman Hong Seok-hyun said, "that we have to take the initiative in the unification of Korea, but only through peaceful measures." The unification of Korea, Hong told his listeners, "is a requirement, not a choice."

Korean Americans' thinking about such great issues is gaining help from their ancestral homeland. Two examples tell vivid stories from a conference organized in November 2017 by Faith & Community Empowerment, or FACE—formerly Korean Churches for Community Development. Action for Korea United, AKU, an organization that comprises eight hundred civic groups in South Korea, came to L.A. City Hall to speak to the City Council and officials of many other groups about realities and hopes in that divided peninsula.[20] Chairman of AKU, In-taek Seo, said the organization is promoting "the Korean Dream of reunification of the Korean people and an end to the tragedy of seventy years of division." They pursue that aim through education programs on the "post–Cold War era" and by collaborating with Korean and international experts. They also create many programs to "help North Korean defectors who have resettled in South Korea but find it difficult to start new lives in a free society after growing up in a state where individual choice and opinions are, in fact, illegal." Seo said there are about thirty thousand such "refugees" from the Democratic People's Republic of Korea (DPRK) in the North to the Republic of Korea (ROK) in the South.

Even more specifically, Kenneth Bae, author of *Not Forgotten*, a stirring book about his 735 days of imprisonment in North Korea, spoke to the L.A. forum.[21] Bae is a Korean American businessman who organized tours of North Korea for years before the totalitarian government turned against him because he was helping Christian missionaries. Bae was born in Seoul in 1968, migrated to the United States with his parents in 1985, and lived in San Jose and Torrance, California. He graduated from the San Francisco Bible College and Covenant Theological Seminary in St. Louis and became a Presbyterian preacher and Southern Baptist minister, working with youth missions internationally. He had been working at Christian tours into North Korea from Dalian and Dandong, China, since 2007 when he was arrested in 2012. The charge against him at trial was simply that by preaching Christian religion "you are spreading lies about our Great Leader and trying to overthrow our government."[22]

So Bae was sentenced to hard labor and endured through illness, hospitalization, and other difficulties for two years. His wife and grown children and his parents kept up petitions to the U.S. State Department and the White House, which responded with attempts to have him freed that were frustrated by the DPRK government until 2014, when Bae was freed and could return to the United States. He wrote *Not Forgotten* to commemorate those who kept vigil and worked to free him. But he is not bitter when he speaks to conferences. Rather, he preaches that South Koreans and Americans should help the ordinary people of North Korea who are suffering malnutrition and worse in an often famine-wracked totalitarian state.

Well, as we all know changes have been dramatic in 2018. North Korea now promises to give up nuclear weapons and the U.S. demands that to happen within a year while it promises the North economic help. Korean Americans are following events closely and hope to see continued progress, even reunification of the nation that has been divided by ideology and war since 1945. Myung Cha, a senior vice president and head of real estate appraisal for Hanmi Bank in Los Angeles sees Korea unifying over time as a "neutral country, a Switzerland for Asia where all countries could get together to solve problems." Cha came to the U.S. as a young boy with his father in 1974. Others in the Korean Community's offspring-of-immigrants generation believe progress will be slower, as economic costs emerge and the bitterness of decades takes time to fade.

Yet happily there is optimism. "We all have relatives in South and North Korea," said Charles Rim, founder of an accountancy firm in

Lomita, California.[23] Chong Ho (Charles) Rim immigrated to the United States in the late 1970s with his father, who was a South Korean consular official. After high school and degrees from UCLA, he founded Charles Rim Accountancy Corp. in 1988. He wants "both sides to get together in Korea, where my wife and I have family," Rim says. "We visit Korea and hope for the best, although naturally we are more involved with our college-age children's education and the economy and other issues here in America."

Thus, looking ahead, we can expect many changes in the neighborhood, from China's growing involvement throughout Asia to emerging unity and peace on the Korean Peninsula and of course to new policies of the United States—and perspectives for Korean Americans.

As to the outlook for Korean Americans, Stewart Kim said, in answering my questions in 2017, that all Americans should not be surprised if South Korea begins to chart a different course for its future as policy differences emerge between it and the United States. "I don't think the special relationship between the U.S. and Korea is quite as special and unconditionally warm as it once was, especially among the younger generations of Koreans," said Kim, who as noted above in this chapter has family and business interests on both shores of the Pacific. "But going the other way, Korean Americans today seem to have greater pride and interest in the country of our ancestors than ever before. They are attuned to all of the issues now confronting Korea, and they care deeply. So, given the rise of China and political waves going on in both South Korea and the U.S., it has become a more nuanced and balanced relationship. And that is for the better I think."

The truth is, Korean Americans will be involved in Korea for years and decades to come and so will the United States, as peace and progress work their way.[24] In the traditional way of immigrants' offspring and descendants, they will visit the land of their parents and grandparents, study its history, and explain it to their children even as they engage their families in issues of the United States and its evolving society.

But in the turmoil of the present, it's a good bet that Korean Americans will lobby and fight as their relatives and forebears reached out to help the Korean community emerge from the isolation of the 1992 L.A. Riots. The challenge then was to work for a "seat at the table" so Korean Americans could be present when decisions were made affecting their community. Today the second great challenge is to campaign for political office and influence—for a hand on the steering wheel—to ensure that the United States does not decline into an isolationist and narrow nation but continues to grow and develop as a model for people of all nationalities, races, and creeds.

As it has been, so it shall be. From the start, this book has taken Korean Americans as examples of people and nations from all over the world who have played their parts in building this America. In chapter 1, Jihee Huh defined the Korean community: "We are a very eclectic people with many talents but most importantly focus on education and hard work as our collective mantra." And we have chronicled the competitive spirit and hard work, the deep faith and the strong commitment, of Koreans over more than seven decades to achieve their American vision.

But seven decades is a short time for this new immigrant group to have come so far. So to sum up, what qualities have enabled the Korean community to adapt relatively quickly and contribute to American life? Was it their competitiveness? Or their Confucian rigor honed by centuries of colonization and poverty? Or is it their sense of obligation and social commitment born of deep religious faith? Obviously it is all of those things plus one more. They have come to the United States even as America is coming to a new understanding of its geography. Previous immigrants from Asia were often denied acceptance. Chinese people came to "Gold Mountain" in the 1850s only to see immigration of Chinese laborers curtailed by the Chinese Exclusion Act of 1882. Japanese-born immigrants could not be naturalized; even their U.S.-born children, who were citizens, were shamefully sent to internment camps during World War II. But Korean immigrants, for all their rude awakening in the 1992 Riots and some continued sullen resistance even today, have been able to educate their children and attain recognition and welcome—as have most Asian Americans today. Los Angeles and California and really all parts of the United States recognize that we are at home in the Pacific World. And the Korean community reminds us all of its vision, hard work, and faith; it is both a piece of the American fabric and a light shining toward America's future.

Notes

Preface

1. Yang Ho Cho, interviews with author, at dinner meeting in 2014 and written interviews in 2015.
2. Yang Ho Cho, interviews with author.
3. Associated General Contractors of America, Survey, January 2017; see also U.S. Bank survey, and Federal Reserve reports.
4. Don Chang, interviews with author, 2017, 2015, and before.
5. Hyepin Im, interviews with author, 2015 and 2017.
6. Sabrina Kay, interview with author, 2016.
7. John Lim, interview with author, April 18, 2016.

Chapter 1. Icon of the Korean Community for L.A.

1. Roger Vincent and Peter Pae, "South Korean Firm Unveils Plans to Put Its Stamp on L.A. Skyline," *Los Angeles Times*, April 3, 2009. Cited with permission.
2. Yang Ho Cho, interview with author, October 28, 2015. (Cho was responding to author's written questions.)
3. U.S. Census Bureau, current population statistics, based on 2013 estimates; Daniel Ichinose, director demographic research, Asian Americans Advancing Justice on 2015 estimates for Koreans in U.S.
4. Jihee Huh, vice president of Pacific American Fish Co., interview with author, February 7, 2016; she was honored by U.S. Congress for testimony on the Comfort Women issue.
5. Edward Taehan Chang, professor of ethnic studies, University of California, Riverside, interviews with author, June 9, 2015, June 22, 2016; also reference his extensive writings in *Korean and Korean American Studies Bulletin* and books.
6. See Michael J. Seth, *A Concise History of Korea* (Lanham, MD: Rowman and Littlefield, 2016), 227–228, for an explanation of the hermit kingdom, in which the function of Korean policies was to keep foreigners out and minimize contact with outsiders.
7. See ibid., 283, for colonial Korea from 1910 to 1945.
8. U.S. Department of Defense, Defense Manpower Data Center, casualty statistics for American War and Military Casualties, Congressional

Research Service, April 28, 2017, table 1, p. 2, "Korean War"; United States and *Encyclopedia Britannica*, statistics for South and North Korea and China.

9. Population estimates for 2018: North Korea, 25,584,307, South Korea, 51,124,318, both from www.worldometers.info, accessed April 11, 2018.

10. Professor Edward Chang, interview with author.

11. Tom Suh, interview with author, November 2015.

12. Young Woo, Young Woo and Associates, interview with author, New York, September 2015.

13. Interview with Yang Ho Cho.

14. Kevin Starr, *Continental Ambitions* (San Francisco: Ignatius Press, 2016), 256; Starr, *California: A History* (New York: Modern Library Edition, a division of Random House, 2005); Starr, *California Dream*, series of eight volumes (Oxford and New York: Oxford University Press, 2005). All inform this book.

15. Yang Ho Cho, biographical material from Korean Air public relations, also with his speeches, including Town Hall, Los Angeles, March 2010. Cho Choong Hoon, material from corporate history, Hanjin Shipping and Korean Air; Cho, *The Economist*, August 31, 2015.

16. Eric Richardson, article on Statler Hotel history, "Looking East on Wilshire Boulevard from Beaudry Avenue, 1954–2010," *Los Angeles Times*, August 6, 2009, cited with permission.

17. James Flanigan, *Smile Southern California, You're the Center of the Universe: The Economy and People of a Global Region* (Stanford, CA: Stanford University Press, 2009).

18. Grace Yoo, interviews with author, June 2015, September 2017.

19. Dr. David Lee, interviews with author, 2001, 2005, 2009; full story printed in Flanigan, *Smile Southern California*, chap. 3.

20. Dr. C.L. "Max" Nikias, author's interviews over years; Nikias, biographical material from University of Southern California.

21. Cho, interview with author.

22. Nikias, interview with author.

23. Cho, interview with author.

24. Dr. Richard Drobnick, USC's International Business Education and Research IBEAR program, teacher of Yang Ho Cho; Malcolm Gladwell, excerpt, "The Ethnic Theory of Plane Crashes," chap. 7 in *Outliers* (Boston: Little Brown, 2008), 179–223, also reprinted in *The New Yorker* magazine, 2008.

25. Gladwell, "Ethnic Theory of Plane Crashes."

26. Brian Lee, interview with author, NetKAL Summit meetings, 2015.

27. Y. H. Cho, interview with author.

28. Myung Oak Kim and Sam Jaffe, *The New Korea: An Inside Look at South Korea's Economic Rise* (New York: Amacom—American Management Association, 2010).

29. Don Kirk and International Herald Tribune, "Kim Blames Family Firm For Korean Air Fatalities," *New York Times*, April 21, 1999.

30. Frank Gibney, *Korea's Quiet Revolution: From Garrison State to Democracy* (New York: Walker and Company, 1992).

31. Choong Hoon Cho, obituary in *New York Times*, November 19, 2002; obituary in *The Economist*, November 28, 2002.

32. *Los Angeles Times*, articles on cargo containers stranded at L.A.–Long Beach ports, Hanjin bankruptcy, August, September, November 2016. Cited with permission.

33. Los Angeles County Economic Development Corp., reports on trade, *LAEDC Economic Forecast* (an annual publication), 2015; Flanigan, *Smile Southern California*.

34. Christopher Martin, chairman, A.C. Martin Partners, interviews with author, September 21, 2015, November 10, 2016.

35. Chris Martin, interview with author.

36. Bill Allen, interview with author, February 2014, at the Big Pour, and in years afterward.

37. Yang Ho Cho, interview with author.

38. David Zuercher, interview with author, January 2017.

39. Dean Marilyn Flynn, USC School of Social Work, interview with author, February 4, 2015.

Chapter 2. Pioneers, Heroes, and Law That Made Asian America

1. Sheila Smith Noonan, *The Changing Face of North America since 1965* (Broomall, PA: Mason Crest Publishers, 2004). The book has forewords by Senator Ted Kennedy and Immigration Agency officials from the United States and Canada.

2. Dosan Ahn Chang Ho, *Dosan: The Man and His Thought*, published in English by Young Korean Academy (Heung Sa Dahn) and online at http://www.newworldencyclopedia.org/entry/Info:Main_Page. (San Francisco: Young Korean Academy, 2005).

3. Woo Sung Han, *Unsung Hero: The Colonel Young O. Kim Story*, translated by Edward T. Chang (Riverside: University of California Riverside, 2011).

4. Dosan, *The Man and His Thought*, 7.

5. Edward T. Chang and Woo Sung Han, *Korean American Pioneer Aviators: The Willows Airmen* (Lanham, MD: Lexington Books, 2015).

6. Dosan, *The Man and His Thought*, 2.

7. John Cha and Susan Ahn Cuddy, *Willow Tree Shade: The Susan Ahn Cuddy Story* (published in the United States by Korean American Heritage Foundation, printed in Seoul, South Korea, 2002); Ann Simmons, obituary for Cuddy, *Los Angeles Times*, July 1, 2015.

8. Quote from Susan Ahn Cuddy, *My Heritage*, video, April 1, 2011, YouTube, https://www.youtube.com/watch?v=rBJcIGWkBVI; see also Cha and Cuddy, *Willow Tree Shade*.

9. Cha and Cuddy, *Willow Tree Shade*, 55.

10. Woo, *Unsung Hero*, 23.

11. Ibid., 24.

12. Woo, *Unsung Hero*, 172 and subsequent.

13. Ibid., 369.

14. U.S. Census Bureau, population of Los Angeles County, 1960.

15. James Flanigan, *Smile Southern California, You're the Center of the Universe: The Economy and People of a Golden Region*, chap. 2, "Ballistic Missiles to Cellular Phones" (Stanford, CA: Stanford University Press, 2009).

16. Margaret Sands Orchowski, *The Law That Changed the Face of America: The Immigration and Nationality Act of 1965* (Lanham, MD: Rowman and Littlefield, 2015), 47, 48.

17. Quoted in ibid., chapter 3, "Making of the Law"; for quotation, see http://www.presidency.ucsb.edu/ws/?pid=26787 for LBJ State of the Union Address 1964.

18. Mrs. Anne Kim, interview with author, October 29, 2016, Houston.

19. Seoul National University, "History," www.useoul.edu/history, 2016.

20. Mrs. Anne Kim, interview with author.

Chapter 3. Newcomers Spur Industry, Earn Place in America

1. Los Angeles County Economic Development Corp. Economic Forecast, February 21, 2018, https://LAEDC.org/event/economic forecast; California Fashion Association, LA Fashion Market 2017, continual reports on website CalFashion.org; Korean American Apparel Manufacturers Association, KAMA, 2015, www.kamainfo.org.

2. Ilse Metchek, president California Fashion Association, interview with author, November 24, 2017.

3. Los Angeles Economic Development Corp.

4. Jung C. Choe, publisher of Pacific Textile News, interviews with author, January 7, 2017, and June 2015.

5. David Kleinman, longtime apparel industry owner and vendor veteran, and other apparel industry owners, interviews with author, 2015 to 2017.

6. Peter Kim, owner Hudson Jeans, interviews with author, November 2016, October 2017.

7. Joe Mozingo, Tiffany Hsu, and Victoria Kim, "Fashion District Firms Raided in Cartel Money Laundering Probe," *Los Angeles Times*, September 10, 2014.

8. Joy Han, owner Joy Group Co. and Voomonline.com website, Joy Han and husband James Kim, company started in 2005, off-shoulder dresses and other apparel, interview with author, 2015.

9. Sung Won Sohn, chairman of Forever 21 (now retired); Do Won Chang, chief executive, and company representatives, interviews with author, 2017, 2015, and before. See also articles in *Forbes, L.A. Business Journal*, and numerous publications dating back over a decade.

10. San Pedro Wholesale Mart.com website, https://sanpedromart.com, visits to Mart; interviews with former *Downtown News* editor and current Los Angeles business editor Jerry Sullivan, 2016, 2017, sanpedromart.com /about.

11. Assessment of the Changs' wealth by *Forbes*, "The 400 Issue, Special Issue 2017," Forbes Media LLC, 400th issue, 2017, and Billionaires issue, 2018.

12. Peter Kim, interview with author.

13. Dr. Chun Bin (Charlie) Yim, interview with author, March 2017; Dr. Chun Bin (Charlie) Yim, *I Will Work for Nothing* (Rancho Santa Fe, CA: self-published, copyright Dr. Chun Bin (Charlie) Yim, 2015).

14. Yim, *I Will Work for Nothing*, 14.

15. Sukhee Kang, interviews with author, October 2016 and 2017–2018; Kang, *The Power of Possibility: My American Journey* (Irvine, CA: Independent Publisher, copyright Sukhee Kang, 2013).

16. Samuel Wurtzel, Alan Wurtzel, Circuit City history and commentary about in *Forbes, New York Times*, 1985; *Wall Street Journal*, 2012; and Kang, *The Power of Possibility*.

17. Peter High, "We All Compete with Amazon," *Forbes* magazine, November 10, 2014, citing Alan Wurtzel's book *We All Compete with Amazon*.

18. Peter Kim, Chun Bin Yim, and Sukhee Kang, interviews with author on the impact of the Los Angeles Riots of 1992.

Chapter 4. Rude Awakening to American Dream

1. Pew Research Center, Social and Demographic Trends, Korean Americans, www.pewsocialtrends.org/fact-sheet/asian-amcricans-koreans-in-the-u-s/.

2. Lou Cannon, *Official Negligence: How Rodney King and the Riots Changed Los Angeles and the LAPD* (New York: Random House, 1997), 112–114. (The first half of this chapter contains many references to this book.)

3. John H. Lee and John Goldman, "Boycott Puts Korean Stores at Center of N.Y. Racial Strife," *Los Angeles Times*, May 20, 1990, account of the Family Red Apple incident.

4. Writings of pioneering Korean American journalist K.W. Lee, K.W. (Kyung Won) Lee Center for Leadership, Los Angeles, "Looking Back In Awe, Living Dangerously in America's Killing Fields," www.kwleecenter .org/writings/lookingbackinawe.{bib}

5. Cannon, *Official Negligence*, 113.

6. PBS.org, *Sa I Gu from Korean Women's Perspectives*, POV film, aired on PBS September 10, 1993, showing women of families who owned stores destroyed in the L.A. Riots of April 29, 1992. (Sa I Gu means 4-2-9.)

7. Edward T. Chang, *Ethnic Peace in the American City: Community Building in Los Angeles* (Riverside: University of California, 1999).

8. Cannon, *Official Negligence*, 108–110, 115–119.

9. Ibid., 152–159.

10. Cannon, *Official Negligence*, 334.

11. PBS.org, *Sa I Gu*.

12. Cannon, *Official Negligence*, 334–347.

13. Ashley Dunn, "Looters, Merchants Put Koreatown under the Gun," *Los Angeles Times*, May 2, 1992.

14. Edward Taehan Chang, "Confronting Sa-i-gu: Twenty Years after the Los Angeles Riots," April 29, 2012, http://yokcenter.ucr.edu/docs/other /11-12_Confronting_Sa-i-gu_Article.pdf.

15. John Lim, founder and managing partner Lim Ruger Law Firm (now LimNexus), interview with author, April 18, 2016.

16. Cannon, *Official Negligence*, 367.

17. Chief Charlie Beck, Los Angeles Police Department, writing in special commemorative page in the *Los Angeles Times*, "The Chief's Promise: The LAPD Will Never Fail the City Again," April 30, 2017.

18. *Korean-American Mosaic: Portraits of a Vibrant Community*, video produced by Network of Korean American Leaders at USC School of Social Work, shown on KoreanAmericanStory.org, January 2010, includes comment by Judge Ryu.

19. Lee, "Looking Back in Awe."

20. John Suh, chief executive of LegalZoom, Inc., interview with author, March 18, 2016.

21. Spencer Kim, chairman CBOL Corp., Pacific Century Institute, interviews with author and meetings at his company and official ceremonies, 2015, 2016, and 2017.

22. Mimi Song, chief executive, Superior Grocers, board leader, Network of Korean American Leaders, interviews with author, 2013, 2015.

23. Hyepin Im, founder and chief executive of Korean Churches for Community Development–Faith and Community Empowerment, interviews with author, July 2015, January 2016, October 2017, and events including participation in Lighting the Community Summit, November 2017.

24. Lee, "Looking Back In Awe."

25. Ibid., 4.

26. Ibid., final lines of essay.

Chapter 5. Entrepreneurial Energy and Deep Faith

1. Phillip Chang, founder and chief executive of Yogurtland, interview with author, August 2015.

2. Stella Lim, owner and designer at Ryu Fashions, interview with author, April 2016.

3. Frank Gibney, *Korea's Quiet Revolution: From Garrison State to Democracy* (New York: Walker and Company, 1992); Gibney, interviews with author, 1980s, 1990s.

4. Gibney, *Korea's Quiet Revolution*, 43.

5. Ibid.

6. Ibid., 17; Michael Schuman, *Confucius and the World He Created* (New York: Basic Books, 2013).

7. Gibney, *Korea's Quiet Revolution*, 43–44.

8. Bruce Cumings, *Korea's Place in the Sun: A Modern History* (New York: W.W. Norton, [1997] 2005).

9. Drobnick, interview with author, 2015.

10. Sabrina Kay, interviews with author, July 2015, May 2016; columns in *Los Angeles Times*, 2006–2007; James Flanigan, *Smile Southern California, You're the Center of the Universe: The Economy and People of a Golden Region* (Stanford, CA: Stanford University Press, 2009).

11. Sabrina Kay, interviews with author, early 2000s–present.

12. Roy Choi, *L.A. Son: Roy Choi, My Life, My City, My Food*, with Tien Nguyen and Natasha Phan (New York: HarperCollins, 2013); coverage in

Los Angeles Times, April 2017, for LocoL, experimental restaurants in Watts and Oakland.

13. Judy Joo, *Korean Food Made Simple* (New York: Houghton Mifflin Harcourt, 2016); Joo, interview with author, October 2017.

14. Danny Lee, interview with author, October 2017, at Council of Korean Americans conference, Washington, DC.

15. Roy Choi, with Tien Nguyen and Natasha Phan, *L.A. Son: My Life, My City, My Food* (New York: HarperCollins, 2013), 227.

16. #LOCOL, http://www.welocol.com/about-us, accessed April 11, 2018.

17. Hannah Pae, "Food for the People: Roy Choi, Locol, and Urban Revitalization," Kollaboration, https://kollaboration.org/6685/food-for-the-people -roy-choi-locol-and-urban-revitalization/.

18. Pae, "Food for the People."

19. Peter and Jihee Huh, interviews with author, February and November 2016, February and April 2017.

20. Sunnie Kim, founder and chief executive, Hana Financial Inc., interview with author, April 2016.

21. John Suh, president LegalZoom, Inc., interview with author, March 2016 and conversations over 2015–2017 at Network of Korean American Leaders meetings.

22. Brian Lee, interview with author, NetKAL Summit meetings, 2015; research on companies he started.

23. The following passages draw from Michael Yang, founder and chief executive Michael Yang Capital Management and companies including Become.com, interviews with author, October and November 2017; date of arrival is from Cumings, *Korea's Place in the Sun*.

24. James Flanigan, column, *Los Angeles Times*, April 10, 1988.

25. Eric Kim, interview with author, at NetKAL Summit, New York, September 2015.

26. Bom Suk Kim, founder of Coupang Global LLC, in Korea, Stewart Kim, managing partner PGP Capital Advisors regarding Coupang, interview with author.

Chapter 6. "We Korean Americans can move this country forward"

Source for chapter title: Jim Yong Kim, president World Bank

1. Je Hoon Lee, director of Network of Korean American Leaders, meetings and interviews with author, 2013 through 2017 (Lee), and with the Korea Foundation, Seoul, 2016.

2. Michael Yang, a cofounder of the Council of Korean Americans, interviews with author, October–November 2017.

3. June Lee, MD, board chair, Council of Korean Americans, interview with author, Washington, DC, October 2017.

4. Daniel Ichinose, director Demographic Research, Asian Americans Advancing Justice website, https://advancingjustice-la.org; Ichinose, interviews with author, 2016.

5. Esther Star Kimm, corporate recruiter, interviews with author, October 2014–2016, 2017.

6. Jerry Kang, professor of law, UCLA, Council of Korean Americans, interview with author and his profile.

7. Yamamoto, Eric K., *Race, Rights, and Reparation: Law and the Japanese American Internment*. 2nd ed. (New York: Wolters Kluwer Law and Business, 2013), n.p.

8. Young Woo, founder Young Woo & Associates, New York, interviews with author, 2013 and 2015, at his company; record of projects.

9. Margarette Lee, partner, Young Woo & Associates, interview with author, New York, September 2015.

10. Kyung Yoon, Kwangsoo Kim, and Raymond John, interviews with author, at NetKAL Summit, New York, September 2015.

11. John Lim, founder LimNexus law firm L.A. and president of the Council of Korean Americans at Summit meeting Washington, DC, 2015; Ronald Reagan Building, Washington, DC, speeches by John Lim and Jim Yong Kim, chairman World Bank.

12. Records of 2016 CKA Summit Meeting in Washington and public positions declared on its website, www.councilka.org.

13. CKA Summit, Washington, DC, 2017, author's reporting and interviews, October 20, 21.

14. Gideon Yu and Il Yeon-Kwon, profiles on Soyoung Ho, "Bankers, Grocers, and Lots of Kims," *Forbes*, January 2, 2009, www.forbes.com and on their own companies' sites, including EVA Automation and the San Francisco 49ers football team for Yu; "Founders Greeting" and nj.hmart.com for Il Yeon-Kwon.

15. South Korea's economy, 2017 statistics from website of Focus-Economics, accessed April 11, 2018, https://www.focus-economics.com/countries /korea; other economic reports that go up through 2016.

16. James Flanigan, author of this book and of articles on Pohang Steel (POSCO), *Los Angeles Times*, July 2009, cited with permission.

17. Finbarr O'Neill, former president Hyundai Motor America, interview with author, October 2015; history of Hyundai Motor told in Myung Oak Kim and Sam Jaffe, *The New Korea: An Inside Look at South Korea's Economic Rise* (New York: American Management Assn., 2010).

18. Samsung's early history is told in Oak and Jaffe, *The New Korea*.

19. Samsung's development of smartphones in collaboration with Qualcomm is told in James Flanigan, *Smile Southern California, You're the Center of the Universe: The Economy and People of a Golden Region* (Stanford, CA: Stanford University Press, 2009).

20. Peter Pae, bureau chief, *Bloomberg News* in Seoul, revolt against chaebol corporate giants and government leaders reported by Pae and *Bloomberg News* in Seoul, 2016, 2017; Pae, interviews with author, April 2015, November 2016–2017.

Chapter 7. Historic Challenges, Beacons for the Future

1. Douglas Lee, chief executive Stanley Prep, Seoul and Beverly Hills–based training school for Korean employees of U.S. companies, interview with author, Seoul, November 2016, and Los Angeles, July 2017.

2. Sam Yoon, executive director, Council of Korean Americans, interview with author, July 2017.

3. COEX Center, Seoul, event drew thousands of young Koreans; I interviewed many there in English or in Korean with assistance of locals.

4. Soh Yeong Roh's presentation was at NetKAL Summit meeting, November 2016, she and others at this presentation, interviews with author.

5. Suok Noh, board chair NetKAL, partner Redbadge Capital, interview with author, November 2016. Author's own presentation to the NetKAL meeting told of the promise for them in partnerships in the United States.

6. Angela Killoren, chief operating officer CJ America, January 2016, interviews with author, January 16, November 2017.

7. Suk Park, cofounder DramaFever.com, interview with author, September 2015, New York; Mark Shaw, chief executive of CJ E & M, interview with author, 2016.

8. Stewart Kim, president PGP Capital, interviews with authors, from 2007 for Flanigan, *Smile Southern California, You're the Center of the Universe: The Economy and People of a Golden Region* (Stanford, CA: Stanford University Press, 2009), and 2013–2017.

9. David Min, lawyer running for U.S. Congress in Irvine, California, and backer Paul Kim, interviews with author, CKA Summit, Washington, DC, October 2017.

10. Daniel Koh, campaign literature; Michael Yang, campaign backer, interview with author, November 2017.

11. David Ryu, member Los Angeles City Council, interview with author, August 2015; Ryu, interviews with author, Korean American events, 2016, 2017.

12. Lim and Yoon, Council of Korean Americans, interviews with author, 2017, on North Korea galvanizing Korean Americans, reflecting change in U.S. Korean community and Korean attitudes toward the United States.

13. Grace Jo, refugee from North Korea, interview with author, at NetKAL Summit 2015, New York.

14. Mike Kim, U.S. rescuer of North Korean women, NetKAL Summit, interview with author, 2013, Los Angeles.

15. Joseph Kim, interview with author, Asia Society and Korea Foundation book signing for *Under the Same Sky*, June 2015.

16. Economic comparisons of North and South Korea, from *Business Insider*, *The Economist* magazine, and author's research of government statistics, 2017.

17. Spencer Kim, interviews with author, 2013–2017.

18. Charles Rangel, former U.S. Congress member, interview with author, 2016.

19. Hong Seok-hyun, chairman Korean media group JoongAng Ilbo; JoongAng Ilbo, *Peace Odyssey: 32 Korean Intellectuals Journey along the North Korea-China Border* (published February 2016 by JoongAng Ilbo, Seoul), about a 2015 journey by thirty-two Korean scholars in pursuit of Korean unification.

20. In-taek Seo, president Action Korea United, interview with author, at Lighting Ceremony by Faith & Community Empowerment at Los Angeles City Hall, November 2017.

21. Kenneth Bae, author of *Not Forgotten: The True Story of My Imprisonment in North Korea* (Nashville: W Publishing, 2016), on his imprisonment in North Korea, interview with author, November 2017.

22. Bae, *Not Forgotten*, 40.

23. Charles Rim, interview with author, April 6, 2018.

24. Author's summation, projections, and hope.

Bibliography

Associated General Contractors of America, Survey, January 2017.

Bae, Kenneth. *Not Forgotten: The True Story of My Imprisonment in North Korea.* Nashville: W Publishing, 2016.

Beck, Charlie, "The Chief's Promise: The LAPD Will Never Fail the City Again." *Los Angeles Times.* Special commemorative page. April 30, 2017.

California Fashion Association. "LA Fashion Market 2017." Continual reports. CalFashion.org.

Cannon, Lou. *Official Negligence: How Rodney King and the Riots Changed Los Angeles and the LAPD.* New York: Random House, 1997.

Cha, John, and Susan Ahn Cuddy. *Willow Tree Shade: The Susan Ahn Cuddy Story.* Seoul: Korean American Heritage Foundation, 2002.

Chang, Edward Taehan. "Confronting Sa-i-gu: Twenty Years after the Los Angeles Riots." April 29, 2012. http://yokcenter.ucr.edu/docs/other/11-12_Confronting_Sa-i-gu_Article.pdf.

———. *Ethnic Peace in the American City: Community Building in Los Angeles.* Riverside: University of California, 1999.

———, and Sung Han Woo. *Korean American Pioneer Aviators: The Willows Airmen.* Lanham, MD: Lexington Books, 2015.

Cho, Choong Hoon. *The Economist.* August 31, 2015.

———. Obituary in *New York Times*, November 19, 2002; obituary in *The Economist*, November 28, 2002.

Choi, Roy, with Tien Nguyen and Natasha Phan. *L.A. Son: My Life, My City, My Food.* New York: HarperCollins, 2013.

Council of Korean Americans. Records of 2016 CKA Summit Meeting in Washington and public positions. www.councilka.org.

Cuddy, Susan Ahn. *My Heritage.* Video. April 1, 2011. YouTube. https://www.youtube.com/watch?v=rBJcIGWkBVI.

Cumings, Bruce. *Korea's Place in the Sun.* New York: W.W. Norton, [1997] 2005.

Dosan Ahn Chang Ho. *Dosan: The Man and His Thought.* Published in English by Young Korean Academy (Heung Sa Dahn) and online at www.NewWorld Encyclopedia.org. San Francisco: Young Korean Academy, 2005.

Dunn, Ashle, "Looters, Merchants Put Koreatown under the Gun." *Los Angeles Times.* May 2, 1992.

Flanigan, James. Column. *Los Angeles Times.* April 10, 1988.

———. *Smile Southern California, You're the Center of the Universe: The Economy and People of a Golden Region*. Stanford, CA: Stanford University Press, 2009.

Focus-Economics, accessed April 11, 2018, https://www.focus-economics.com /countries/korea.

Forbes. "The 400 Issue, Special Issue 2017." Forbes Media LLC. 400th issue, 2017, and Billionaires issue, 2018.

Gibney, Frank. *Korea's Quiet Revolution: From Garrison State to Democracy*. New York: Walker and Company, 1992.

Gladwell, Malcolm. "The Ethnic Theory of Plane Crashes." Chap. 7 in *Outliers* (Boston: Little Brown, 2008), 179–223; also reprinted in *The New Yorker* magazine, 2008.

High, Peter. "We All Compete with Amazon." *Forbes* magazine. November 10, 2014.

Ho, Soyoung, "Bankers, Grocers, and Lots of Kims." *Forbes*. January 2, 2009. www.forbes.com.

Hong, Euny. *The Birth of Korean Cool*. New York: Picador USA, 2014.

Ichinose, Daniel. Director demographic research. Asian Americans Advancing Justice on 2015 estimates for Koreans in United States. https://advancing justice-la.org.

Joo, Judy. *Korean Food Made Simple*. New York: Houghton Mifflin Harcourt, 2016.

JoongAng Ilbo. *Peace Odyssey: 32 Korean Intellectuals Journey along the North Korea-China Border*. Published February 2016 by JoongAng Ilbo, Seoul.

Jung, Francine, "Food Truck Legend Roy Choi Introduces Healthier Fast Food." January 25, 2016. *Korea Bizwire*. koreabizwire.com/food-truck-legend -roy-choi-introduces-healthier-fast-food/48765.

Kang, David C. *East Asia before the West: Five Centuries of Trade and Tribute*. New York: Columbia University Press, 2010.

Kang, K. Connie. *Home Was the Land of Morning Calm*. Cambridge, MA: Da Capo Press, Perseus Books Group, 1995.

Kang, Sukhee. *The Power of Possibility: My American Journey*. Irvine, CA: Independent Publisher, copyright Sukhee Kang, 2013.

Kim, Joseph. *Under the Same Sky: From Starvation in North Korea to Salvation in America*. Boston: Houghton Mifflin Harcourt, 2015.

Kim, Mike. *Escaping North Korea: Defiance and Hope in the World's Most Repressive Country*. Lanham, MD: Rowman and Littlefield.

Kim, Myung Oak, and Sam Jaffe. *The New Korea: An Inside Look at South Korea's Economic Rise*. New York: Amacom–American Management Association, 2010.

Kirk, Don, and International Herald Tribune, "Kim Blames Family Firm For Korean Air Fatalities." *New York Times*. April 21, 1999.

Korean American Apparel Manufacturers Association (KAMA), accessed 2015, www.kamainfo.org.

Korean-American Mosaic: Portraits of a Vibrant Community. Video. Produced by Network of Korean American Leaders at USC School of Social Work. Shown on KoreanAmericanStory.org. January 2010.

Lee, Chang-Rae. *Native Speaker*. New York: Riverhead Books, 1995.

Lee, Erika. *The Making of Asian America*. New York: Simon and Schuster, 2015.

Lee, Helie. *Still Life with Rice*. New York: Touchstone-Simon and Schuster, 1996.

Lee, John H., and John Goldman, "Boycott Puts Korean Stores at Center of N.Y. Racial Strife." *Los Angeles Times*. May 20, 1990.

#LOCOL. http://www.welocol.com/about-us. Accessed April 11, 2018.

Los Angeles County Economic Development Corp. Reports on trade. *LAEDC Economic Forecast* (an annual publication). 2015.

———. *Economic Forecast*. February 21, 2018. https://LAEDC.org/event /economic-forecast.

Min, Pyong Gap. *Caught in the Middle: Korean Communities in New York and Los Angeles*. Oakland: University of California Press, 1996.

Mozingo, Joe, Tiffany Hsu, and Victoria Kim. "Fashion District Firms Raided in Cartel Money Laundering Probe." *Los Angeles Times*, September 10, 2014.

Noonan, Sheila Smith. *Korean Immigration: The Changing Face of North America since 1965*. Broomall, PA: Mason Crest Publishers, 2004.

Orchowski, Margaret Sands. *The Law That Changed the Face of America: The Immigration and Nationality Act of 1965*. Lanham, MD: Rowman and Littlefield, 2015.

Pae, Hannah, "Food for the People: Roy Choi, Locol, and Urban Revitalization." *Kollaboration*. https://kollaboration.org/6685/food-for-the-people-roy -choi-locol-and-urban-revitalization/.

Park, Sukza. *River Junction Tales of Life in the United States and Korea*. CreateSpace Independent Publishing Platform, 2015.

Pew Research Center, Social and Demographic Trends, Korean Americans, www.pewsocialtrends.org/fact-sheet/asian-americans-koreans-in-the-u-s/.

Plate, Tom. *Conversations with Ban Ki-Moon*. Singapore: Marshall Cavendish Editions, 2012.

Richardson, Eric, "Looking East on Wilshire Boulevard from Beaudry Avenue, 1954–2010." *Los Angeles Times*. August 6, 2009. Cited with permission.

Sa I Gu from Korean Women's Perspectives. POV film. Aired on PBS September 10, 1993. PBS.org.

Schuman, Michael. *Confucius and the World He Created*. New York: Basic Books, 2013.

Seth, Michael J. *A Concise History of Korea*. Lanham, MD: Rowman and Littlefield, 2016.

Seoul National University. "History." 2016. www.useoul.edu/history.

Simmons, Ann. Obituary for Susan Ahn Cuddy. *Los Angeles Times*. July 1, 2015.

Starr, Kevin. *California Dreams*. 8 vols. Oxford and New York: Oxford University Press, 2005.

———. *California: A History*. New York: Modern Library Edition, a division of Random House, 2005.

———. *Continental Ambitions*. San Francisco: Ignatius Press, 2016.

Takaki, Ronald. *Strangers from a Different Shore: A History of Asian Americans*. New York, NY: Back Bay Books / Little Brown [1989] 1998.

U.S. Census Bureau. Current population statistics. Based on 2013 estimates.

———. Population of Los Angeles County. 1960.

U.S. Department of Defense. Defense Manpower Data Center. Casualty statistics for American War and Military Casualties. Congressional Research Service. April 28, 2017. Table 1, p. 2, "Korean War."

Vincent, Roger, and Peter Pae, "South Korean Firm Unveils Plans to Put Its Stamp on L.A. Skyline." *Los Angeles Times*. April 3, 2009.

Wada, Haruki. *The Korean War: An International History*. Lanham, MD: Rowman and Littlefield, 2014.

Woo, Sung Han. *Unsung Hero: The Colonel Young O. Kim Story*. Translated by Edward T. Chang. Riverside: University of California, 2011.

Worldometers.info, population date, accessed April 11, 2018.

Yamamoto, Eric K. *Race, Rights, and Reparation: Law and the Japanese American Internment*. 2nd ed. New York: Wolters Kluwer Law and Business, 2013.

Yim, Dr. Chun Bin (Charlie). *I Will Work for Nothing*. Rancho Santa Fe, CA: Self-Published, 2015.

Yoo, Grace J., and Barbara W. Kim. *Caring across Generations: The Linked Lives of Korean American Families*. New York: New York University Press, 2014.

Yu, Eui-Young, Hyojoung Kim, Kyeyoung Park, and Moonsong David Oh. *Korean American Economy and Community in the 21st Century*. Los Angeles: Korean American Economic Development Center, 2009.

Index

About the Author

JAMES FLANIGAN, as business columnist for the *Los Angeles Times, New York Times*, and other publications, has covered national and international business and economics for fifty-three years. For twenty years he wrote a column in the business section of the *Los Angeles Times*. Since 2005, he has written on small business for the *New York Times*. During eighteen years with *Forbes* magazine, he served as bureau chief in Washington, Los Angeles, London, and Houston and later in New York as assistant managing editor. He started as a financial journalist at the *New York Herald Tribune* in 1963. His work has won numerous awards, including the Gerald Loeb Lifetime Achievement Award for Distinguished Business and Financial Journalism and the John Hancock Award for Excellence in Business Journalism. His book *Smile Southern California, You're the Center of the Universe* tells of Southern California's vibrant business climate and its relation to the global economy. He has also completed the *Biography of Henry Segerstrom and the Evolution of Orange County Society*.

Flanigan, who was born in New York City, is a history and English graduate of Manhattan College. He and his wife, Patricia, have five adult children and an assortment of exuberant grandchildren.